STRAIGHT STITCH
MACHINE APPLIQUÉ

History, Patterns & Instructions for this Easy Technique

Letty Martin

Plate 1. *PATIO POTS, 57" X 74".*

Martin, Letty.
     Straight stitch machine appliqué : history, patterns &
instructions for this easy technique / Letty Martin.
          p.   cm.
     Includes bibliographical references.
     ISBN 0-89145-839-5 : $16.95
     1. Machine appliqué.   2. Machine appliqué--Patterns.   3. Quilts
I. Title.
TT779.M37   1994
746.46--dc20   94-38946
                                                              CIP

Additional copies of this book may be ordered from:

American Quilter's Society
P.O. Box 3290
Paducah, KY 42002-3290
@16.95. Add $1.00 for postage and handling

Dedication

This book is dedicated to my husband Bill
for his encouragement and constant belief
in my ability to complete this project.
This book is also dedicated to my parents,
Anna and Rex Richardson.
Mother taught me to sew at a very young age
and both of my parents provided me
the opportunity to continue sewing and learning as I grew.

"Thanks to my mother's tender care
For she materials did prepare
and taught my hands to sew."
From an Ohio sampler by Eliza Ann Bruen, 1826.

Plate 2. *DRESDEN PLATE QUILT, 72" x 90".*

Acknowledgments

Thanks are due to many people who encouraged, helped, and supported my efforts in writing this book. Thanks to my husband Bill, to my parents Anna and Rex Richardson, to my son Douglas who was my computer consultant and chief photographer, and my son Scott who was my color consultant. To the memory of my mother-in-law, Mary Martin, who always encouraged me to do my best. To Jeanne Colwell and Pam Riesing, then associated with Mountin Mist, who initially encouraged me to pursue the idea of writing this book. To Gretchen Tatge, who gave me the opportunity to teach these straight stitch machine appliqué concepts at her shop, Quilt-n Friends, and to my wonderful students who so enthusiastically tried this antique appliqué technique. To great friends who were a source of inspiration and comfort: Carol Grossman, Sandy Deesen, Dorothy Arnold, Carol Van Sickle, Joyce Fogler, Sharon Finton, Jeanne Colwell, Patty Gagnon, and Mindy Beveridge.

A SPECIAL NOTE

On Labor Day, September 7, 1992, lightning hit our home starting a fire which caused extensive damage. As is often the case, what the fire did not burn, the water or the terrible smoke ruined. The manuscript for this book was done, as were all the quilts. Everything survived, but, some of the quilts were subject to severe smoke damage.

When I first became interested in quilting, a friend had the color fade in a quilt she was working on, which was displayed on a quilt rack close to a door wall, even before finishing the quilting. I remembered this and formed the habit of always folding my quilts with the back on the outside. As a result, most of the smoke damage was confined to the back side of the quilts. This and the fact that many quilts were in some kind of a bag, such as a pillow case, really spared them from extensive damage. Several quilts were lost though. Quilts in the areas where the fire was most intense were intact, but, they were very brittle and fell apart when touched. Please consider how you store your quilts and make changes if necessary.

My fabric collection, which was stored in a closet on shelves with the doors closed, also suffered extensive smoke damage. There are companies which specialize in cleaning smoke damaged goods, however they did not really want to tackle my quilting fabrics and it would not have been cost effective to clean anything under one yard in length. Think of all the smaller pieces of fabric you have, all the quarter yards you have bought. Your fabric collection is a very valuable asset; not only should you consider its initial cost but its replacement cost and what it might cost to clean in a similar situation.

The quilting community is truly wonderful! Friends took all my smoke damaged quilting fabric and distributed it to those quilters who were willing to wash it, trying to get rid of the smoke smell and stains. The smell is now gone but not all the stains. Since we quilters cut our fabric into small pieces I can work around those stained areas. My quilt fabric loss was kept to a minimum due to the kindness and caring of the quilting community, especially those ladies in the Oakland County Quilt Guild and the patrons of Quilt-n Friends Quilt Shop. They are truly angels of mercy and I thank them all from the bottom of my heart for their support.

Table of Contents

CHAPTER ONE
HISTORY OF STRAIGHT STITCH MACHINE APPLIQUÉ

Plate 3. *OHIO ROSE, 72" x 89½".*

No historical look at machine appliqué would be complete without examining the role that the sewing machine played in women's lives. The sewing machine was a technological advancement that helped free women from one of the household drudgeries: the responsibility of making her family's clothing and bedding. All the clothing and bedding were usually made by hand, ready-made clothing not being available. The sewing machine, widely available by the 1860's, was a wonderful time saver in this never ending task, and women were quick to adapt their sewing skills to include the sewing machine. In Hearts and Hands, Pat Ferrero comments: "A Kansas woman in the 1860's estimated she could sew more in a day on her new machine than in a week by hand."[1] She adds, "Where (sewing) machines were scarce in pioneer regions they were shared, with women visiting each other's homes and spending the night to get their sewing done."[2] Providing specific information about the effects of machine use, she writes, "Estimates by historians today are that a calico dress that took six and one-half hours (to sew) by hand took fifty-seven minutes by machine, and a man's shirt one hour as opposed to fourteen." She adds, "The time saved was indeed considerable."[3]

However, the sewing machine also encouraged a woman to experiment with making more elaborate clothing. She could be more stylish as she had some extra time to spend on sewing. The sewing machine let the seamstress make tucks, ruffles, pleats, and other decorative details on her clothing in less time than hand sewing. Even after the Civil War when ready made clothing became more available for men and later children, women were still making their complicated fitted dresses at home.

Quilt tops were frequently pieced on sewing machines when one was available researcher Suellen Meyer suggests "...women probably made many machine quilted, utility coverings."[4] Quilt historian Jonathan Holstein claims that "about half of the quilts we have seen which date from the 1860's on are machine pieced."[5]

Suellen Meyer comments: "It is difficult to determine how many nineteenth-century quilts have visible machine stitching in the appliqué or quilting. Such quilts are much rarer than quilts which include machine piecing."[6] She continues, explaining that when machine quilting, "no doubt seam-

Plate 4. Detail of SINGLE TULIP IN A STREAK OF LIGHTNING. Illinois c. 1880. Machine appliquéd and quilted with white thread using very small stitches. All the blocks are machine appliquéd and very uniform in size. Brown print backing. Collection of the author.

Plate 5. *DUTCH TULIPS, 84¾" x 77½". Appliqué. Rutherford County, c. 1890. Cotton: green, red, yellow-orange on white, muslin back; red binding on the straight; quilted by the piece in concentric rows of diamonds, and diagonal rows with red, green, and white thread. Maker: Mother of Mrs. Sharber. Collection of Mildred Locke.*

stresses found it difficult to control the three layers of top, batt, and lining while treadling the machine, for the working space was shallow and the thread often broke. Once adept, however, some turned their attention to their fine quilts, where the visible stitch testified to their skill."[7] See Plate 4.

Women also tried creating appliqué quilt tops using the sewing machine. Jonathan Holstein comments, "...some appliqué quilts are also machine worked, but they are the exception."[8] Appliqué is generally considered to be more time consuming than piecing to produce quilt tops. Appliqué quilts were often "best" quilts reserved for show or guests, while pieced quilts were utilitarian in nature. Some late nineteenth-century quilt makers "used their sewing machines to appliqué since this allowed them to show off both their

machines and their skill."[9] DUTCH TULIPS is a Tennessee quilt that was appliquéd entirely by sewing machine in the 1890's. Bets Ramsey, author of *The Quilts of Tennessee*, comments, "The maker was very skillful in using a straight machine stitch to appliqué all parts of this dramatic quilt. Her placement of the blocks, with the four flowers in the center is ingenious."[10] See Plate 5.

Suellen Meyer comments on the skill required for such machine appliqué: "Machine sewing required practice, as a California woman discovered in 1860...'The wheel made a revolution forward, and then came back with great facility; my work moved the wrong way; the cotton became mixed up in a lamentable manner, and when I endeavored to pull the work into place, crack! went the needle.... Early on Monday morning I was again at work, and had the happiness of actually making stitches.' Such time-consuming practice proved worthwhile. The machine not only stitched ordinary items quickly, but it also served as an important status symbol."[11] See Plate 6, page 10.

A North Carolina quilt made in the 1880's by Joyce Shearin Coleman was appliquéd and quilted by machine. See Plate 7, page 11. In *North Carolina Quilts*, Ruth Haislip Robertson comments, "Surprisingly, this 1880's quilt was entirely made by machine, quilted one block at a time, in the quilt-as-you-go technique. Presumably the maker basted together all layers of each block (with appliqué edges turned under) and then machine appliquéd and quilted the blocks one at a time; next she joined the blocks and machine appliquéd the gold strips of sashing on top of the seams."[12] Ruth Haislip Robertson continues by adding that Genoa Rox Hunter's quilts "displayed a decided degree

Plate 6. *"Photographer Butcher documented the settling of Nebraska in the 1880's with fifteen hundred portraits of frontier families. A folklorist ahead of his time, Butcher also collected the stories of life within the walls of the simple sod houses he photographed. Many of the families chose to drag their sewing machines outside for these portraits, a fact which says a great deal about how important that tool was to ordinary nineteenth-century Americans." An 1888 photograph of the W.H. Blair house at Huckleberry. near Broken Bow, Nebraska, by Solomon Butcher. Solomon D. Butcher Collection/Nebraska State Historical Society, Lincoln. Hearts and Hands, p. 37.*

of creativity."[13] Her PEONY quilt, "began as an eight pointed star and was transformed by machine appliqué stems and leaves into a flower."[14] Her PEONY quilt was made ca. 1880. See Plate 8.

Many of the books which survey state quilts contain examples of quilts which have been straight stitch machine appliquéd. Careful reading and study of these books can uncover some real treasures. *Nebraska Quilts & Quiltmakers* by Patricia Cox Crews and Ronald C. Naugle, shows an original design quilt that is a particularly fine example. Henrietta Yinger designed and made this handsome dark blue, dark red, and green quilt called, LOVE APPLES AND TULIPS in 1883. See Plate 9. The authors comment: "Appliqué quilts of this type called for a maker's

finest workmanship. This maker chose to display her exceptional skill with a sewing machine; the quilt is entirely machine appliquéd. No evident attempts have been made to simplify the design for machine sewing.

The design is very balanced and well proportioned. A central wreath of leaves surrounds the maker's chain stitched signature and the date – 'Etta Yinger. October 24, 1883.' Four triple branched tulips grow from the wreath, balancing the small urns of tulips on the sides and filling the space between the large blocks. Two similar tulips grow from a blue ground in the four corners.

"The urns that hold the large love apples and the smaller urns are in unusually good proportion to their contents. They

Plate 7. *TULIP, 1880's, Churchill community near Macon, Warren County, by Joyce Shearin Coleman (1844–1917). 71" x 89". Collection of Luch Coleman Pope. North Carolina Quilts, p.72.*

Plate 8. *PEONY, ca. 1880, Wake County, by Genoa Rox Hunter Freeman (1849–1905). 74" x 82". Collection of Claire and Doris Freeman. North Carolina Quilts, p. 119.*

are also unusual in their two color design, suggesting a terra-cotta pot inside a navy cachepot, on a red base. The smaller urns have a similar inner liner on a smaller scale."[15]

Michigan Quilts: 150 Years of a Textile Tradition by Marsha MacDowell and Ruth D. Fitzgerald, also shows an especially stunning STAR OF BETHLEHEM quilt with straight stitch machine appliquéd floral motifs in the corner and side triangular pieces around the central star design. This quilt was made by a Native American woman from Leelanau County, Michigan, Mrs. Ogahmahgegedo, in 1912. The star and floral motifs shown on this quilt are typical of the Ottawa Indian designs which "mimic designs depicted in earlier porcupine quill work and beaded pieces of the

Plate 9. *LOVE APPLES AND TULIPS, 1883 (marked). Made by Henrietta Yinger (1860–1924). Probably made in Hanna City, Peoria County, Illinois, and brought to Clay County Nebraska. Collection of De Etta Chatterson Edgar. Cotton, 70" x 70". NQP 3394. Nebraska Quilts and Quiltmakers, p. 93*

Plate 10. *Mrs. Ogahmahgegedo. STAR OF BETHLEHEM (Indiana Quilt) made 1912, Ahgosatown, Leelanau County, Michigan. Collection of Florence Lackie Hender. Cotton with cotton filling, 65" x 75", MQP 86.489. The STAR OF BETHLEHEM pattern is known to have been made by two Native American women from Leelanau County, Michigan. According to James M. McClurken, co-author with James A. Clifton and George L. Cornell, of People of the Three Fires: The Ottawa, Potawatomi, and Ojibway of Michigan, the star and floral motifs exhibited in these two quilts are typical components of Ottawa designs. Each square and triangle formed against the white background by the center star is filled with floral designs that embellish the central design and mimic designs depicted in earlier porcupine quill work and beaded pieces of the same region. It is probable that Native Americans began quilting after the Grand Traverse Mission period; the first person who was recorded to have had furniture in his home, and thus have a need for domestic furnishings such as quilts, was Agosa, who lived on Old Mission peninsula during the mid 1840's. The owner of the quilt, Florence Lackie Hanes, writes that her father, Walter Lackie, acquired it "as a trade for some farm goods. Always treasured by the family, and never used (it is) just called the Indian Quilt." The quilter was known to the family as Mrs. Ogahmahgegedo, but further research has revealed that she may also have been known as Catherine or Jenny Steele. She lived in a settlement known as Ahgosatown, located between Omena and Northport, Michigan. Michigan Quilts, p. 83.*

same region."[16] The colors are especially rich and vibrant in this wonderful quilt, the maker adapting the designs from another source to be used on a quilt. See Plate 10.

Quiltmakers frequently mixed hand appliqué and machine appliqué techniques. An exuberant large tulip quilt made by Stella Jenkins of North Carolina in 1888 had "three of its blocks appliquéd by hand, one by machine."[18] See Plate 11. *Missouri Heritage Quilts* shows an exquisite appliqué quilt made in 1889 by Laura E. Lynes, which features a large central hand appliqué design of Love Apples and Rose surrounded by a "wider meandering vine border which was meticulously stitched down with fine treadle machine straight stitch."[19] See Plate 12. Suellen Meyer points out that "Most sewers found it more difficult to handle

Plate 11. *TULIP, dated 1888, Roundtree community, Pitt County, by Stella Jenkins Jenkins (1869–1944). 78" x 78". Private collection. Made in red and green (a popular nineteenth-century color scheme) with four large blocks. It is unusual, however, that the maker initialed and dated her quilt in the center "SMJJ1888." The elaborate border of appliquéd swags and stars is also out of the ordinary. One block is appliquéd by machine, the other three by hand. Blocks are defined by a narrow green piping. North Carolina Quilts, p. 74.*

curves and points with a machine than by hand."[20] Perhaps they let their chosen design dictate which method was used.

In twentieth century quilts there are frequent examples of combined sewing techniques, machine appliqué and machine piecing. Machine appliquéd handles are seen on baskets, and stems on such patterns as English Ivy and North Carolina Lily and other similar patterns. These handles and stems were easy and quick to machine appliqué as they involved no points or sharp curves. Many DRESDEN PLATE and FAN patterns also were appliquéd using the sewing machine. See Plate 13 and 14 (Plate 14 is on page 14). These simple patterns lend themselves readily to straight

Plate 12. *LOVE APPLE AND ROSE. Missouri Heritage Quilts. p. 12.*

Plate 13. *FAN QUILT. Machine appliquéd c. 1930. Photo: Letty Martin.*

stitch machine appliqué.

Some common ingredients found in all these appliqué designs is their simplicity of shape, large pieces, broad points, and gentle curves. These guidelines can help us when selecting designs to machine appliqué. The 1930's SUNBONNET SUE has these design features, large uncomplicated pieces and gentle curves. Probably the maker, Lola Lois Jenkins of Kansas, folded under the edges of the appliqué pieces, basted them in place and then using the straight stitch, machine appliquéd them to the background blocks. She went on to embroider each bonnet with its own unique design. See Plate 15 (page 14). Straight stitch machine appliqué, while a time saver compared to the time needed to hand appliqué a block or quilt, was not the only reason women chose to use their sewing machine. If time saved were the only factor involved in the choice of appliqué techniques, why would the maker spend so much time beautifully embroidering the bonnets? I suspect liking the look of the finished appliqué block and showing off sewing skills were some other reasons for choosing to machine appliqué the SUN-BONNET SUE blocks.

Appliqué quilt designs allow for a wide range of creative expression. By using the simple techniques developed to help you straight stitch machine appliqué, you can create beautiful, traditional looking appliqué quilts. With practice and patience you will soon be mastering curves and points while showing off your mastery of the sewing machine just as were the resourceful and creative ladies 100 years ago.

Plate 14. *DRESDEN PLATE. Machine appliquéd, c. 1940. Collection of Vicki West.*

Plate 15. *SUNBONNET SUE, c. 1930. Lola Lois Jenkins, Hazelton, Kansas. Machine appliquéd with cotton thread in colors to match the fabric. Hand embroidery on the bonnets and a running stitch outlines each appliqué piece. Hand quilted.*

CHAPTER TWO
STRAIGHT STITCH MACHINE APPLIQUÉ

Plate 16. *THE OAK LEAF AND REEL QUILT, 61" x 80".*

This section describes the materials, tools, and techniques necessary for you to successfully accomplish straight stitch machine appliqué. Refer to this section when getting ready to appliqué or for a review on how to prepare the various pieces for appliqué such as leaves, stems, vines, and circles. Use this material for guidelines to adapt patterns found elsewhere. The pattern section, shows projects to get you started on straight stitch machine appliqué. They have been identified by skill level, as beginner or intermediate. Your initial project might be a small one, such as a pillow or wall hanging. Remember that old adage, practice makes perfect. When learning a new technique, do not be too hard on yourself. If your first attempt is not as perfect as you might like, your second attempt will be much better. Adapt the patterns and ideas to suit your needs: bed sizes, color preferences, and design ideas. Feel free to combine border ideas and blocks in combinations other than those I have shown. The quilt projects are successful as presented, but are also presented as ideas to stimulate your creativity.

The last section, Finishing the Quilt, describes exactly that how to assemble and finish your quilt. How to appliqué a straight stitch machine appliqué border, determining what length to make your borders, as well as corner treatments will be discussed. Stretching the quilt, marking it for quilting designs, and binding the quilt's edges are also covered. All the information needed to make a quilt, specifically a straight stitch machine appliqué quilt, is included. Have fun quilting and let your creativity come forth!

Supplies needed for straight stitch machine appliqué are cotton fabric, your sewing supplies, iron and ironing board, and sewing machine plus

> freezer paper,
> cotton swabs,
> starch or sizing,
> small cup,
> appliqué foot for sewing machine,
> fine transparent nylon thread.

ALL THOSE WONDERFUL FABRICS

Fabric which is 100% cotton gives the best results in appliqué projects. Cotton fabrics will keep a crease and not spring back the way a blend of polyester and cotton will. Cotton fabrics are readily available in a wide variety of colors and designs. Prints range from tiny calicos to large scale flower and geometric designs. Solid color cotton fabrics are also easy to find in a range of colors and color gradations. Since many appliqué designs are of flowers, having a range of colors to work with can be important.

Many appliqué patterns are done with all solid color fabrics. This gives a crisp, neat look, especially if there is sufficient contrast between the colors used in the block design. A softer, more blended look can be achieved by using colors close in value. See the ROSE OF SHARON block in solid colors, Plate 17.

The same ROSE OF SHARON block shown in Plate 19 takes on a new look with some print fabrics. When using several prints in a block, try to vary the size or scale of the printed design. This adds interest to the block as well as separates the different appliqué pieces.

Plate 18. *Rose of Sharon with large scale prints. Photo: Douglas Martin.*

Plate 17. *Rose of Sharon in solid colors. Photo: Douglas Martin.*

Try using some of the newer large scale floral and geometric prints in your appliqué blocks. The large scale patterns take on a completely new look when cut into smaller pieces. See Plate 18.

Background fabrics for appliqué

Plate 19. *Rose of Sharon with some print fabrics. Photo: Douglas Martin.*

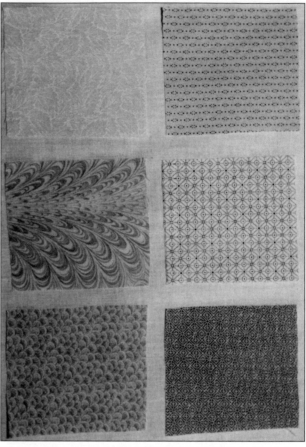

Plate 20. *Background fabrics. Photo: Douglas Martin.*

designs have traditionally been bleached or unbleached muslin. Muslin gives the most contrast between the block design and background. See Plate 17.

Different colors of background fabrics can give a new look to a favorite pattern. It may take a little more work to get the proper contrast between the appliqué design and the background. You can create a different look in your quilts by using a light, medium, or dark color background fabric. See Plate 19 and the ROSE WREATH quilt, page 47.

Consider using a printed fabric for the background in your appliqué blocks. Choose a fabric which will not compete with the appliqué design. Many of the light beige printed fabrics or white on white designs can be substituted for a plain muslin or white background. Almost any light colored print fabric could be used for the background. Small geometric prints are another possible choice. Some fabrics are shown to help guide you in choosing the background fabric for your blocks. See Plate 20.

The subtle interest that a print fabric adds to your block can also give a new look to a favorite appliqué design. See PATIO POTS on page 1, DRESDEN PLATE crib quilt on page 39, and the PINEAPPLE quilt on page 46 for quilts using printed background fabrics.

All these variables, solid or print fabrics, large or small scale prints, whether used in the appliqué design or background fabric, can energize an appliqué design. Try some of these other ways to use your fabrics and create a truly unique quilt.

PREWASH YOUR FABRICS

Prewash your fabrics to remove sizing and prevent bleeding of the dye. Wash in cool water with a phosphate free detergent. To help reduce raveling before washing, make a ½" clip parallel with the selvage at each end of the fabric. See Figure 1. Set your washing machine for a slow agitation speed and short wash time, three to four minutes.

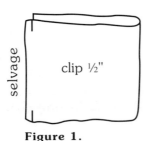

Figure 1.

Red colored fabrics seem particularly prone to dye bleeding. It would be a good idea to wash them by hand so you can see if this is a problem. If there is a lot of bleeding, a rinse of one cup clear vinegar to two cups water may succeed in stopping the dye's bleeding.

Dry your fabrics in the dryer until almost dry. Remove and fold, hand pressing to remove wrinkles. Finish by air drying. If you are ready to use the fabric right away, press with a warm iron. Many fabrics look so good after hand pressing that it is hard to tell they have been washed. The clips next to the selvage will reduce raveling as well as remind you the fabric has been washed and is ready to be used.

PLANNING YOUR QUILT BLOCKS

Cut out the pieces of your appliqué design in the colors you have selected and pin them to the background fabric. Stand back and look at the block. Is there sufficient contrast in the colors and design scale of the selected fabrics to let the individual parts show? Does the block look like you wanted it to? If not, recut and change the pieces you do not like. Keep trying different colors and printed fabrics until you are satisfied with the arrangement of fabrics and colors in your sample block. Pin the block where you can see it as you go about your work. If you still like it after 24 hours, great! This will be the master plan for the blocks in your quilt.

In addition to standing back to look at the sample block, here are some other tips to help you see what the block really looks like, rather than what you think it looks like. Squint while looking at the block; this will help you to see the distribution of the lights and darks. Hold the block up in front of a mirror and look in the mirror at the block. It may look different than you imagined. Look at the block through your camera lens; often you will see secondary patterns you have created. If the block is not symmetrical, turn it upside down and look. Rearrange and recut parts as necessary. Try one or all of these techniques to help see your block more clearly and achieve just the right look.

THREAD

There are several important things to consider when choosing the thread you will be using in straight stitch machine appliqué. Since the appliqué will be sewn in place using the sewing machine and visible thread, it is important to choose a thread that will be noticed as little as possible. You do not want the line of stitching to detract from your appliqué design. Cotton thread in a color matching the appliqué fabric works well. Using a fine, transparent nylon thread as the top thread on the sewing machine and cotton thread on the bobbin is preferred. The nylon thread becomes almost invisible, blending in with the colors in the appliqué fabric.

Fine, transparent nylon thread gives the least visible line of stitching, especially on solid color fabrics. The thread comes in two colors, clear and smoke. Clear, transparent nylon thread should be used with light and medium color fabrics, while the smoke color should be used with medium and dark color fabrics. If the clear thread is used with dark colors you will see light reflected off the line of stitching. On the other hand, if you use the smoke color thread on light color fabrics, there will be a shadow. This would be especially noticeable on solid color fabrics. The transparent nylon thread works especially well on printed fabrics as it blends in with all the colors present.

You will want to choose a transparent nylon thread that is fine and soft. Quilt shops are the best retail store in which to purchase this very fine, transparent nylon thread. There are other stores selling transparent nylon thread but the thread will not necessarily be as fine and soft as that sold in quilt shops. There are some mail order companies listed in the back of this book which are good sources of quilting supplies, including transparent nylon thread.

Most sewing machines will be able to sew with this very fine thread. Since this thread is stretchy you may need to loosen the upper tension on your sewing machine in order to have a balanced stitch. First, record the tension setting your sewing machine normally uses. You will need to know the correct tension setting to reset the machine when you have finished with the straight stitch machine appliqué. Thread your sewing machine with transparent nylon thread on top and cotton thread in the bobbin. Sew a test line of stitching on a scrap of fabric. If the stitching looks pulled, loosen the tension setting. Continue to experiment until the stitch is correctly balanced. Now, make a note of this tension setting. This will let you quickly make the necessary tension adjustments when you next use transparent nylon thread.

Cotton or a cotton covered polyester thread is a good choice for the bobbin thread. The bobbin thread should match or blend in with the color of the fabric you are going to appliqué. If the color of the bobbin thread does not match or blend, you will get a dotted look on top of the appliqué piece as you sew. When beginning a project, I wind a bobbin for each of the thread colors needed to match the fabric appliqué pieces I am using in my quilt.

Cotton thread can also be used as the top thread. You may decide to use cotton thread as a top thread on the sewing machine for several reasons. First, your machine may have difficulty sewing with the nylon thread. Second, you might not be able to purchase the fine, transparent nylon thread where you live. Third, you may prefer the look of one type of thread over another.

Cotton thread color should closely match that of the fabric to be appliquéd, whether it's the needle or bobbin thread. Selecting thread one shade darker than the appliqué fabric will often make the stitching less noticeable, although your appliqué stitch will be more visible on solid color fabrics if using a top thread which is cotton. You will need as many different color threads as fabric colors to be appliquéd. If using print fabrics, match the background color of the print.

Choose a good quality cotton or cotton covered polyester core thread which has been made with long staple fibers for strength and durability. Threads which I have found to be very good are Coats and Clark's Dual Duty® and Super Sheen®, and Mettler's Silk Finish® cotton thread. Dual Duty® is a thread with a polyester core, covered with cotton, while the Super Sheen® is an all cotton thread. There is a wider range of colors in the Dual Duty® than the Super Sheen® thread. Mettler's Silk Finish® cotton threads also come in a wide range of colors. Less expensive threads are made with short fibers. They are weaker and will fray and break more easily. Always choose the best quality materials available to you, whether choosing thread, fabric, or batting. Making a quilt is a time intensive project. The time that you will invest calls for the use of quality materials.

DESIGNS THAT WORK FOR STRAIGHT STITCH MACHINE APPLIQUÉ

Many appliqué designs can successfully be machine appliquéd using the straight stitch. Patterns that will be easy to appliqué have: 1) pattern pieces which are medium to large in size, 2) gentle curves, 3) leaves and other points that are broad, and 4) not too many pattern pieces. Many of the appliqué designs from the nineteenth and early twentieth centuries fit this description. These will be easy-to-appliqué designs whether you sew them by hand or with the sewing machine. Slim pointed leaves, small pieces, and tight curves are all areas that are more difficult to successfully appliqué. See Figures 2 and 3.

Figure 2. *Difficult to appliqué.*

Figure 3. *Easy to appliqué.*

Very often you can easily redraft an appliqué piece to meet the above guidelines without changing the character of the pattern. Let's redraft the flower shapes shown in Figure 2. Fold a 5" square of paper into eighths. Measure 2" along each straight edge from the bottom point. Mark. (Figure 4). Now cut the paper in a gentle curve between the marks. Open the paper flower you have just cut. The petals should be more gently curved than in our example. The new shape will be easier to appliqué than our example with the deep tightly curved petals.

Leaves can also be changed for easier appliqué. Once again we will redraft the leaf in our example. Fold a 2" square of paper in quarters. Draw and cut a new plump curved line. See Figure 5. Open the paper. Repeat until the point is broad and you like the shape. This new leaf will be easy to appliqué, and does not really change the appliqué pattern very much.

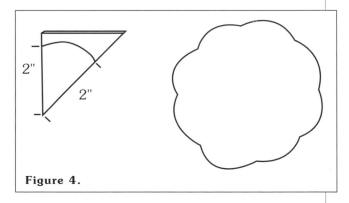

Figure 4.

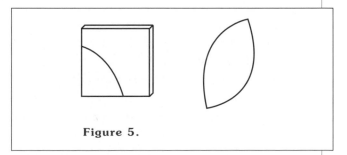

Figure 5.

THE SEWING MACHINE

A clean, lint free, and oiled sewing machine will give the best results when appliquéing and constructing a quilt top. Refer to your sewing machine manual for specific instructions on how to maintain your machine. For safety's sake, before beginning any maintenance, unplug your sewing machine. Generally, areas you will need to pay attention to are the bobbin case and under the throat plate around the feed dogs. These areas accumulate a lot of lint from the fabrics. The lint needs to be brushed away. Remove any threads that have gotten caught in the bobbin area. If your sewing machine is not sewing with a balanced stitch or has some other problems, take it to your nearest dealer for the necessary adjustments. You will be amazed at how well your machine sews when it is properly adjusted and lint free!

SEWING MACHINE NEEDLES

It is important to begin each quilt project with a new sewing machine needle as well as a clean and lint free machine. A new needle is sharp and will pierce the fabric easily.

Sometimes when sewing over a straight pin the needle will nick the pin, which causes the needle to become blunt, dull, or even bent. These conditions can cause sewing problems. For these reasons remove pins before you sew over them. In fact, I like to pin the appliqué pieces to the background block in the middle of the piece rather than at the edge, to prevent such problems. The sewing also moves along more smoothly if you do not have to stop and remove pins.

After sewing a big project or several small projects, your needle will not be as sharp as when you began and should be replaced with a new, sharp needle. The best appliqué results from using a new sewing machine needle at the beginning of a project.

SEWING MACHINE FEET AND THROAT PLATES

An appliqué foot gives the best results

when using the sewing machine to appliqué. This foot has a raised area on its underside. The raised area under the foot lets it glide smoothly around the appliqué pieces, especially corners which have several layers of fabric. It also has toes that are far apart, letting you see what and where you are sewing. There are two types of appliqué feet: closed toe and open toe. It is possible to use a regular presser foot, but it tends to get caught on pointed areas where there are several extra fabric layers. Look in your sewing machine manual to see a picture of the appliqué foot for your machine. See Figure 6.

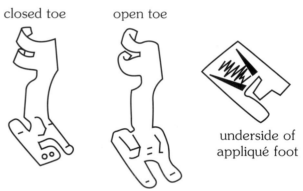

closed toe   open toe

underside of appliqué foot

Figure 6.

A throat plate for straight stitching, which has a small round hole, gives the best support to your work. Some sewing machines only have a throat plate for the zigzag stitch. This has a larger oval opening to allow the needle to move from side to side when sewing a zigzag stitch. In many instances this throat plate will give good results. If you feel the appliqué fabric has too much up and down movement, try covering part of the oval opening with a piece of transparent tape, reducing the opening size. If you have a straight stitch throat plate, switch to this, but remember to change back to the one with the oval opening the next time you use a zigzag stitch.

My favorite combination of appliqué

foot and throat plate is a closed toe foot used with the straight stitch throat plate. This seems to give the best results: your work is supported, yet you can see where to sew. Other combinations that work quite well are using the closed toe foot with the zigzag throat plate or the open toe foot with the straight stitch throat plate. I have found the open toe foot used with the zigzag throat plate when doing straight stitch machine appliqué lets the edge of the appliqué fabric have too much movement. It then becomes harder to sew close to the edge of the appliqué piece and sometimes puckering can be a problem.

APPLIQUÉ TEMPLATES

Two sets of templates will be needed. One set will be cut from template plastic, another set from freezer paper. Template plastic is an opaque or clear sheet of thin plastic through which you can easily see to trace the pattern pieces needed for your appliqué design. It is also easy to cut. Plastic templates are used as pattern pieces for the fabric and for the freezer paper pressing templates. Template plastic is available in most quilt shops.

Place the template plastic over the appliqué pattern pieces and trace the shapes needed for your pattern. There are two exceptions: stems and circles. You will not need a plastic template for stems. How to make stems using freezer paper will be described later. Circles can be cut from any thin cardboard such as poster board.

Using paper scissors, cut out the appliqué shapes on your traced line. Trace and cut smoothly and accurately because these shapes represent the finished appliqué shape. Label the top of each piece as it is traced from the pattern and, when appropriate, indicate the piece will be reversed by adding the letter R. For exam-

ple, a leaf shape might be labeled BR. This means it is piece B and will be traced around on the wrong side of the fabric with the label side down. Also it will need to be turned over so the label side is up, away from the fabric when traced around. When the fabric is cut out, the leaves will face in opposite directions. Usually pieces which are reversed are asymmetrical, but not all asymmetrical pieces need to be reversed. Let your pattern be your guide.

Circles are most accurate if a compass or some type of template is used to duplicate the size needed. Tracing around coins may also give accurate small circles, if the size is correct. There are templates of various size circles you can buy, usually at an art or office supply store. These are very nice to have on hand. You will find just tracing a circular pattern does not give a very round template shape no matter how carefully you work. Use the compass, coin, or circle template to draw the circle pattern right on a piece of cardboard. Thin cardboard such as a file folder or poster board makes a good template for circles. We will be pressing fabric around the circle template and need the extra rigidity cardboard provides. Template plastic can melt so is not the best choice of materials in this instance. Carefully cut out this circle template as this will be the finished shape of your circle. You will not need freezer paper circles, only this thin cardboard template.

There is a plastic template material available called Templar® which can withstand heat. If you are using Templar® only one set of templates would need to be cut. You could use these templates as patterns for cutting out as well as for pressing the fabric. Templar® is usually available at quilt shops or through one of the mail order sources listed at the end of the book.

FREEZER PAPER TEMPLATES

Freezer paper is used to wrap foods before freezing. There are two kinds of freezer wrap available for purchase. One is a clear plastic wrap and the other a plastic coated paper. The freezer wrap we are interested in for straight stitch machine appliqué is the plastic coated paper. Freezer paper can generally be purchased in grocery stores and the kitchen sections of hardware or variety stores.

The plastic coated (shiny) side of the freezer paper is useful to us in preparing our appliqué pieces for sewing. Finished size templates will be cut from the freezer paper. These freezer paper templates will be placed on the wrong side of the fabric appliqué shapes, shiny side up and the seam allowance of your fabric appliqué pieces will be pressed back over the freezer paper templates. The edge of the freezer paper template acts as a fold line for the fabric. The plastic coating will help hold the seam allowance in place when pressed.

To make freezer paper templates, place a plastic template on the paper side of the freezer paper and trace around it. Multiple layers can be cut from the freezer paper at one time. Place the piece of paper with your pattern on top of several other pieces of freezer paper. Pin to securely hold all the layers together and cut on the traced lines. You can cut out up to four layers of freezer paper at one time. Freezer paper has a right and wrong side just as fabric does. Make sure the paper side is facing the same way on all pieces or some templates will be reversed.

Several freezer paper templates of each shape will be needed. Planning to use each freezer paper template about four times, cut as many as your pattern requires. For example, if your pattern calls for 16 leaves you would cut four freezer paper leaf templates. You can use each freezer paper template until the edges become bent and you lose the original shape. It then becomes time to use a new freezer paper template.

Stems require only a freezer paper template. Cut a strip of freezer paper the finished width of the stem or vine and about 12" long.

Cut out all of the freezer paper templates needed for the shapes in the block. You can then prepare all these pieces for appliqué at one time and be ready to machine appliqué an entire block.

CUTTING OUT FABRIC APPLIQUÉ PIECES

There are several things to consider before cutting out the fabric appliqué pieces. First, place the plastic templates on the wrong side of the fabric, label side facing the fabric's wrong side. Place the template so any curved areas will be on the bias. See Plates 21 and 22, page 25. This lets the seam allowance easily stretch or shrink when pressed back. Sometimes it will not be necessary to clip into the seam allowance, especially on very gentle concave curves placed on the bias. However, be sure to look at the design of the fabric. Perhaps there is a flower you would like to center on an appliqué piece, or there may be stripes you would like to have run vertically or horizontally. If these kinds of situations occur, let them be the first guide as to how the templates are placed on the fabric. When the fabric is a solid or an all-over print so there are no design elements to be used in special ways, place the templates on the fabric with the curved areas on the bias. See Plates 21 and 22.

A sandpaper board is a great help when transferring the appliqué shapes to the fabric. Placed under the fabric, it grips the fabric and keeps it from stretching as you trace around the plastic template. To make

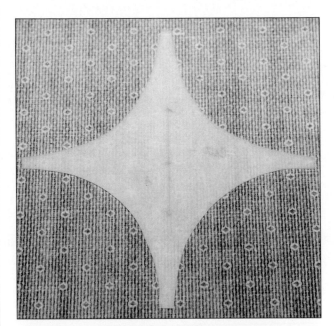

Plate 21. *Curved area on bias. Photo: Douglas Martin.*

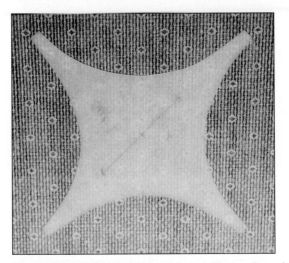

Plate 22. *Curved area on bias. Photo: Douglas Martin.*

your own sandpaper board, you can glue a piece of sandpaper to a piece of masonite board which is the same size. This sandpaper board also makes a nice work surface for handwork. You can also just slip a new piece of very fine sandpaper under your fabric to keep it from stretching.

Once you have decided how to best position the shape on the designs in the fabric, place a plastic template, label side down, on the wrong side of the fabric and trace around it. When you place the templates label side down on the wrong side of the fabric, the shapes will appear just as you traced them from the pattern. Some templates, which you marked with an R, need to be reversed. For reverse shapes, turn the templates over having the label side facing you. This marked line is the finished size of the appliqué. When you cut the piece out you will need to add the seam allowance. Cut out each fabric appliqué piece adding a scant ¼" seam allowance. Most people are familiar with a ¼" seam allowance and a scant means barely as much as indicated. If you have several shapes to cut from the same piece of fabric such as leaves, remember to leave about ½" between the shapes as you trace around the template for the seam allowances. You can cut multiple layers of fabric, usually up to four layers if your scissors are sharp. Stack the layers of fabric, leaving the layer with the marked shapes on top. Pin through all layers, and carefully cut out the shapes adding a scant ¼" seam allowance. Remember to layer your fabrics so all right sides face in the same direction or some appliqué pieces will be reversed.

While cutting multiple layers speeds up the process of getting ready to appliqué, those fabric designs you want used in special ways are best cut as a single layer. Strips and other designs can be better centered or controlled by cutting separate pieces rather than multiple layers.

Stems and vines require strips of fabric cut three times the finished width of the stem or vine. Almost without exception, I like to cut these strips on the bias. Stems and vines are usually curved and the bias has the ability to bend smoothly. The vine bordering REEL SAMPLER was cut on the bias so it could bend to form this graceful

Plate 23. *Reel Sampler. Photo: Letty Martin.*

Plate 24. *Patio Pots. Photo: Douglas Martin.*

border. See Plate 23. PATIO POTS uses a striped fabric. Since the flower stems were straight, these fabric stems were cut on the straight grain to best use this design element. See Plate 24.

Now that the fabric appliqué shapes are cut out, prepare the fabric for straight stitch machine appliqué.

GETTING YOUR WORK AREA READY

Set up your ironing board at a comfortable height, about waist high. Have a dry iron heating on a wool-cotton setting. A small iron with a sharp point is easiest to use. A custard cup or measuring cup with starch or sizing, a cotton swab, and a small pair of scissors are the items you will need to complete your work area.

PREPARING APPLIQUÉ PIECES

Select a fabric appliqué piece, placing it

right side down on the ironing board. Center a corresponding freezer paper template, shiny side up, on the wrong side of the appliqué piece. See Plate 25. With the tip and inner edge of the iron, carefully press the fabric seam allowance over the freezer paper template. Try to press an area on one

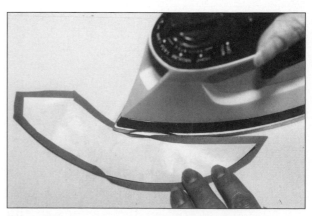

Plate 25. *Pressing seam allowances. Photo: Douglas Martin.*

side and then the opposite side to help keep the template centered. The plastic coating on the paper will soften and help hold the seam allowance in place as it cools.

PRESSING POINTS

If the appliqué piece has points, press the outer tips before the inner corners, if there are any. First, try to determine what kind of point the piece has. There are two kinds of points which require slightly different ways of pressing. See Figure 7.

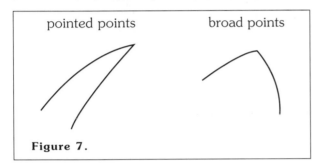

pointed points   broad points

Figure 7.

Narrow points need a mitered fold. First, using the iron, fold and press the fabric seam allowance over the tip of the freezer paper. Trim the seam allowance beyond the tip to 3/16". If there are inner corners, clip into the fabric's seam allowance to within two to three threads of the freezer paper template. Then fold and press in each side. Trim off any additional excess seam allowance that seems to hinder a smooth fold, especially in the tip. However, do not trim the seam allowance to less than 1/8". You want to leave enough seam allowance that it will be caught during machine appliquéing. See Plates 26 – 28.

Broad points require only two folds: first one side, then the other. See Plate 29. If you are unsure which type of point you have, first compare them to the drawings. If you are still unsure, try the two fold method. If the fabric is not folded so it is completely on the back of the appliqué piece you need

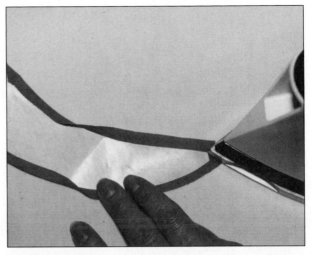

Plate 26. *Pressing a narrow point. Photo: Douglas Martin.*

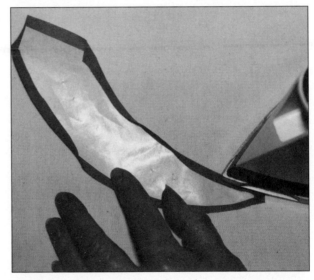

Plate 27. *Pressing the sides of a narrow point. Photo: Douglas Martin.*

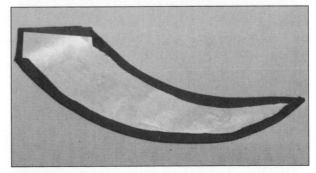

Plate 28. *Pressed narrow point. Photo: Douglas Martin.*

Plate 29. *Photo: Douglas Martin.*

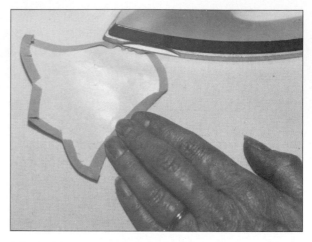

Plate 30. *Pressing smoothed curve edges. Photo: Douglas Martin.*

the mitered fold for narrow points. Carefully release the seam allowance with your finger nail and re-press using a mitered fold.

PRESSING CURVES

Pressing convex curved edges, or those that curve out, involves easing in the fullness which is present when the seam allowance is turned back. If there are peaks or pleats when you press in the seam allowance, use your fingernail to release the seam allowance, redistribute excess fabric, and re-press for a smooth edge. One student reported she likes to use a wooden cuticle stick for releasing the seam allowance from the freezer paper, claiming she did not have long enough fingernails. Pleats pressed in the seam allowance create peaks on the folded edge. You want to have smooth curved edges. See Plates 30 and 31.

Inner or concave curves usually require two or three clips into the seam allowance so the fabric can be pressed back. The exception might be a very gentle curve on the bias. An example is the center section in the PINEAPPLE quilt. The curved edges of the center section of the OAK LEAF

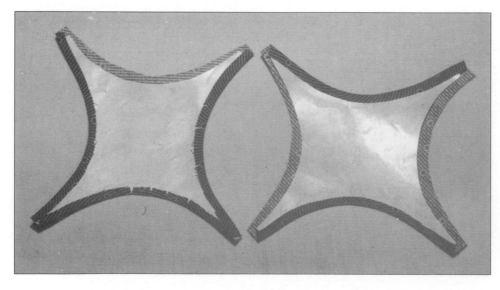

Plate 31. *Clipping a curved seam allowance. Photo: Douglas Martin.*

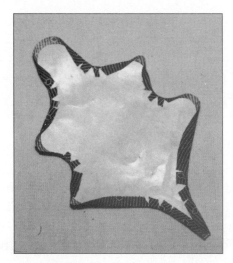

Plate 32. *Trim the seam allowance. Photo: Douglas Martin.*

AND REEL (Plate 31) are deeper and need to be clipped to within two or three threads of the freezer paper template. This is true. whether the curve is on the bias or straight grain. Press.

Remember, broad gentle curves are easiest to press, such as those in the center section and moon shaped pieces of the OAK LEAF AND REEL. The curves in the Oak Leaf of that same pattern are deeper and may require a slightly more narrow seam allowance so they can be pressed

smoothly. If necessary, trimming the seam allowances to a scant ³⁄₁₆" may help with the pressing. See Plate 32.

SPRAY STARCH OR SIZING

Sizing can be used to help seam allowances stay in place when preparing pieces for appliqué. After you have pressed the fabric appliqué piece around the freezer paper template, painting seam allowances with a small amount of sizing and pressing them again will ensure that they stay as pressed. Curved areas and points always need the extra staying power that sizing can give. Pour or spray a small amount of sizing in a custard or measuring cup. Use a cotton swab dipped in the sizing to paint the seam allowance. See Plate 33. Roll the cotton swab around the sides of the container to remove excess sizing so you are using only a little. Try not to saturate the area. Press until dry, turning the appliqué over and pressing on the front side if necessary. See Plate 33. Curved areas almost always need to be painted with sizing. Extra fabric is being eased in when you press a seam allowance back on itself in a curved area so it sometimes wants to spring back.

Plate 33. *Applying sizing to seam allowance. Photo: Douglas Martin*

Sizing helps the seam allowance to stay where you press it. If seam allowances stay pressed under, straight stitch machine appliqué will be easy.

STEMS AND VINES

Center the freezer paper strip that is the finished width of the stem in the middle of a strip of bias fabric. Have the shiny side of the paper facing up. Press one side of the fabric completely over the freezer paper strip, then press the other side. Let cool. Carefully remove the freezer paper strip and move it down the fabric if needed, repeating the pressing process. See Plate 34. Having the stem folded in thirds makes it easy to machine appliqué in place with no seam allowances popping out during sewing. It will be easy to bend the bias fabric strip to follow the curves that a stem or vine may have.

Plate 34. *Pressing a stem in thirds. Photo: Douglas Martin.*

PRESSING CIRCLES

Trace around the circle template on the wrong side of your fabric. Cut out, leaving a ¼" seam allowance. On large circles, sew a row of gathering stitches in the middle of the seam allowance. Use either the sewing machine and the longest stitch length or sew by hand. If using the sewing machine, have the right side of the fabric next to the feed dogs. Leave long enough tails on the thread for gathering. Put the plastic template over the wrong side of the fabric and pull up the bobbin thread, gathering the fabric around the circle template. See Figure 8. Evenly distribute the fullness and press. Let cool and remove the template. Appliqué in place using the straight stitch on your sewing machine.

Smaller circles the size of coins are more easily prepared for appliqué by tracing the shape on the wrong side of the fabric and cutting it out with the ¼" seam allowance. By hand, sew a small running stitch in the middle of the seam allowance, and then pull up to fit around your template. Press and let cool. Remove template and appliqué in place using the straight stitch on your sewing machine.

Remember the shape of the template will be the shape of your prepared fabric appliqué piece. If your circle template has flat edges, so will your appliqué piece, so be sure the circle is perfectly round. This technique for preparing fabric can give you perfect circles every time!

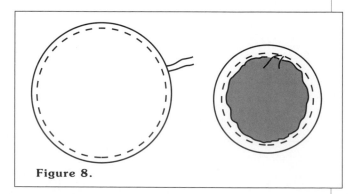

Figure 8.

GET READY TO MACHINE APPLIQUÉ

Good preparation of the appliqué pieces is an important step toward successful straight stitch machine appliqué. What your appliqué pieces look like after being pressed is very much how they will look after being sewn. We need to be sure the seam allowances will stay turned under, the points are pointed, and curved edges are smooth.

Prepare all the appliqué pieces needed for one block. When you are ready to straight stitch machine appliqué a fabric piece to the background block, carefully remove the freezer paper. Use your finger-nail, a long straight pin, or wooden cuticle stick to carefully release the seam allowance from the freezer paper. See Plate 35. If all the pieces are not appliquéd at one time, leave the freezer paper on and they will be ready to use when time allows. The freezer paper prevents the seam allowance from fraying.

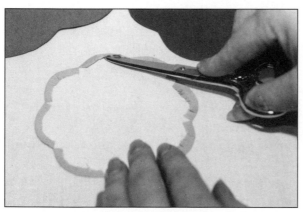

Plate 35. *Releasing the seam allowance from the freezer paper. Photo: Douglas Martin.*

Cut the background blocks the size indicated in the individual quilt patterns. Fold the blocks into quarters and finger crease each fold line. Open up and fold on each diagonal, finger creasing the fold lines. See Figure 9.

These temporary fold lines will help you center the background fabric over the pattern and accurately align the two. When marking the placement of the leaves on the OAK LEAF AND REEL block, you only need a dot along the diagonal crease line

to mark where the leaf ends. The leaf is centered along the diagonal fold line and you will have already marked where its base joins the other two pieces.

A writing tool that will be helpful for marking the placement of the appliqué pieces is the Berol® Verithin silver pencil, which does not smear, shows up on most colors, and washes out easily. Lightly mark only key areas to help you place the appliqué pieces, using dots or dashes. Mark the tips of leaves, where pieces join together, and use dashes for the curving lines of stems or vines. It is better to mark lightly and sparingly, not leaving dark placement marking lines on the background fabric. You can always put the background block back over the pattern and re-mark or double check where an appliqué piece goes. This approach is better than to heavily mark the placement of each piece with your pencil and not be able to cover all the lines with the appliqué.

Depending on the size of the appliqué block you may be using as your guide a complete block pattern, a quarter of a pattern, or a scale diagram of a larger

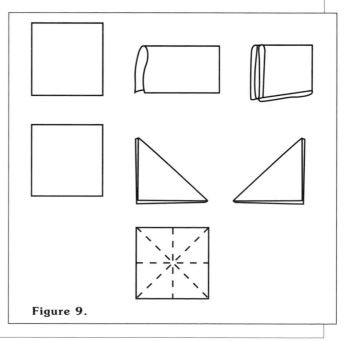

Figure 9.

appliqué block with measurements to help you place the appliqué pieces. If there is a complete block pattern, center the background block over the pattern, matching centers and corners. Pin together and lightly mark with dots or dashes those key points to help place the appliqué pieces.

If there is a quarter of a pattern, match the center and fold lines showing a quarter of the block. Pin to hold in place. Lightly mark key areas. Remove pins and rotate the block a quarter turn, repin, and mark. Continue rotating and marking the block until the entire block is marked. See Figure 10.

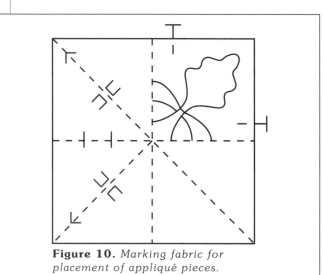

Figure 10. *Marking fabric for placement of appliqué pieces.*

If a dark or printed background fabric is difficult to see through to trace the placement lines, first pin the block to the pattern. Then tape the block to a glass door or window; with the light shining through you will be able to see the design. If you have one, use a light table to mark the background.

You probably have some equipment at home that will let you set up a light table if you wish. A glass topped table with a lamp under it will work as will glass shelves. You can also pull open a dining table and cover the opening with a clean

storm window. Any light table will make it easier for you to mark your fabric, especially larger blocks and borders.

For large blocks there may not be a pattern to trace. Refer to the diagram for measurements to help you make a large size block of your own. Freezer paper is wide and could be used as a large piece of paper on which to draw your master block. Once there is a master block, you can then proceed as described above and all of your blocks will be uniform.

MAKING A MASTER PATTERN

To make your master block, on paper draw a square the size indicated in your pattern instructions. Fold paper as shown in Figure 9, page 31. Trace around appliqué pattern pieces to make a master block.

STRAIGHT STITCH MACHINE APPLIQUÉ THE BLOCKS

The order of appliqué on a block requires that the pieces on the bottom layer be appliquéd first. Usually stems and wreath shapes are appliquéd first, leaves that are behind flowers are next, and finally flowers. Remember to wind bobbins to match each color that you will use in the appliqué before beginning. If using transparent nylon thread, you may need to loosen the upper tension and set the stitch length at 10 to 12 stitches per inch.

Pin the stems in place and straight stitch machine appliqué close to the edge. On curved stems and vines, stitch the shorter, inner curve first. The bias will stretch to fit the larger outer curve.

Straight stitch close to the edge of the appliqué piece. See Plate 36.

Sew slowly and evenly. Start sewing on stems from cut end to cut end. Begin sewing other pieces in areas that are covered by another piece. Finally, there will be

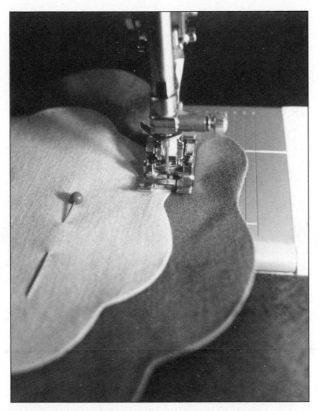

Plate 36. *Straight stitching close to the edge. Photo: Douglas Martin.*

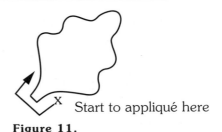

Figure 11. X Start to appliqué here

the last piece which must be completely sewn around. Pick the least visible spot to start and stop sewing. On flowers such as the 1930's Tulip that spot is where the stem and flower meet. This is a gently curving area and seems least conspicuous.

Always start sewing about ½" away from a corner, never at the corner. On the Oak Leaf which is the final piece sewn in place, begin sewing on the stem about ½" away from the corner. Individual leaves are more accurately appliquéd in place if you begin sewing before the point. Frequently these leaves are next to a stem or vine and will remain closer if you begin sewing toward the stem or vine. See Figure 11.

Generally it is easier to have a smooth beginning and ending when it is on straight or gently curving areas.

There are several ways you can end the machine stitching: back stitching, shortening the stitch length, or leaving long tails and hand tying the thread on the back of the block. The type of thread used as the upper thread may be the deciding factor. Transparent nylon thread can be secured either by back stitching or by shortening the stitch length. It will be almost impossible to tell where you started and stopped sewing. Shorten the last half inch of sewing overlapping the thread where you began to sew.

However, cotton thread shows up more used in either of these ways, especially on solid pastel colors. Back stitches might be acceptable on dark print fabric with dark thread color. If cotton thread is used as the upper thread, leave long thread tails. Pull the threads to the back and tie the threads in a knot. Thread a needle with the tails and weave them into the background fabric behind the appliqué, close to the stitching line. This is visually the most pleasing way to secure a cotton top thread.

As you are sewing, remind yourself that slow sewing on the sewing machine is still much faster than sewing by hand! Once you feel comfortable with the technique of straight stitch machine appliqué, you should be able to cut your sewing time in half. Straight stitch machine appliqué is fast and gives a traditional look to your appliqué. From a short distance away it is almost impossible to tell that the appliqué technique used was machine sewing. People will be amazed that you can appliqué so beautifully using your sewing machine! You will like the look and appreciate the time savings.

Plate 37. *Units of a layered flower. Photo: Douglas Martin.*

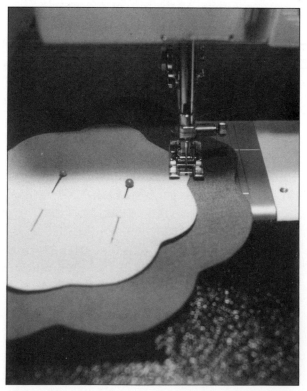

Plate 38. *Stitching a layered flower. Photo: Douglas Martin.*

TIPS FOR A PROFESSIONAL LOOK

Some flowers are built up with layers of fabric. These need to be appliquéd first and then the finished flower unit appliquéd to the background block. The Rose of Sharon is an example of a layered flower. See Plates 37, 38, 39, 40, 41, for how to construct a layered flower. As you appliqué the layers together, trim the background fabric from behind the top layer of fabric. This helps to keep colors clear and eliminates several layers of fabric to quilt through once you are at that stage of the quilt.

A light color placed over a darker color gives an uneven color to the light fabric,

Plate 39. *Photo: Douglas Martin.*

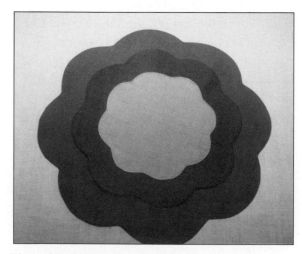

Plate 40. *Photo: Douglas Martin.*

Plate 41. *Back of a layered flower showing background fabric trimmed away. Photo: Douglas Martin.*

Plate 43. *Trimming flower pieces to prevent shadowing of dark fabrics. Photo: Douglas Martin.*

Plate 42. *Stem shadowing through flower fabric. Photo: Douglas Martin.*

Plate 44. *Photo: Douglas Martin.*

creating shadows. The usual situation, for example, would be a stem end showing through a light color flower. Solid, pale fabrics may give the most problems with shadowing. For a uniform color, trim away the stems in the following manner. Pin the flower securely in place. Mark on the stem, with the silver pencil, where the stem and flower meet. Lift the flower and trim away the extra stem, leaving about ³⁄₁₆". Lower

flower and recheck for shadowing. Trim a little more if necessary, but try to leave at least ⅛" of stem. Appliqué the flower in place. See Plates 42, 43, 44.

Keep your work neat! Trim off top and bobbin threads as they are sewn. This keeps them from getting caught in other seams. You will also want to be sure that all threads are trimmed off before stretching the quilt because dark threads can show through a light background fabric.

Plate 45. *FAN QUILT, 1988. Straight stitch machine appliqué. Hand quilted. Barbara Luginhill.*

Trim off ends of the nylon thread as you sew. They are easiest to find as they are sewn. Keeping your work neat on the back lets you be more accurate and neat on the front.

Plate 46. *TULIP BOWL, 1988. Straight stitch machine appliqué. A Mountain Mist pattern #41. Hand quilted. Letty Martin.*

Plate 47. *WINTER MOON, 1990. Original design. Machine appliqué and hand quilted. Sharon Finton.*

Plate 48. *BUTTERFLIES crib quilt, 1987. Straight stitch machine appliqué. A Mountain Mist pattern #33. Letty Martin.*

Plate 49. *WINDBLOWN TULIP pillow slip. Lancaster, Pennsylvania, c. 1920. Machine appliquéd with the straight stitch, 19¼"x29". Collection of Gwen Marston.*

Plate 50. *HEARTS & GIZZARDS or DUTCH ROSE. An experiment to see if one could be successful in appliquéing this type of block which is traditionally pieced. Yes, easily! 1990. Letty Martin.*

Chapter Three
GALLERY OF QUILTS

Plate 51. *DRESDEN PLATE CRIB QUILT, 30" x 39".*

Plate 52. *SINGLE TULIP IN A STREAK OF LIGHTNING, 85" x 93".*

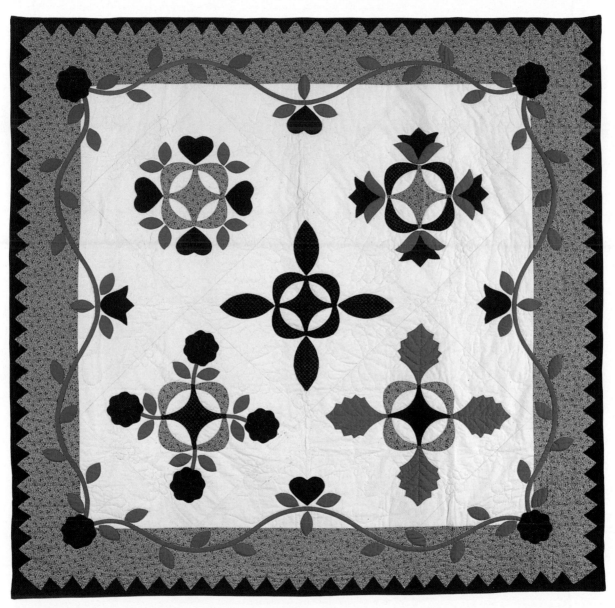

Plate 53. *REEL SAMPLER, 56½" x 56½".*

Plate 54. *1930'S TULIP, 62" x 82".*

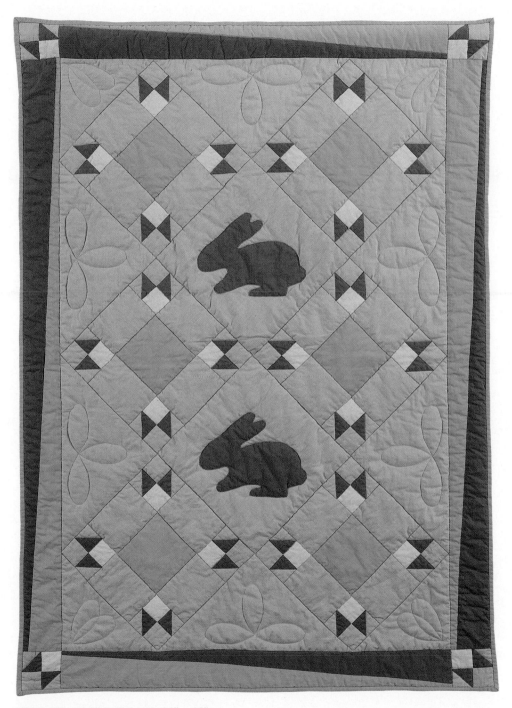

Plate 55. *RABBIT'S PAW, 34" x 48".*

Plate 56. *WHIG ROSE, 82" x 82".*

Plate 57. *FLORAL MEDALLION, 91" x 103".*

Plate 58. *PINEAPPLE, 56½" x 56½".*

Plate 59. *ROSE WREATH, 48" x 48".*

Plate 60. *DOUBLE PEONY AND ROSE, 88" x 107".*

CHAPTER FOUR
PROJECTS AND PATTERNS

Plate 61. *WHIG ROSE WALLHANGING, 46" x 50".*

Patio Pots

57" x 74"

LEVEL: EASY

Color photo on page 1.

Patterns have been rated easy or inter-mediate. This is to guide you to a successful start. With careful workmanship you will soon master the technique of straight stitch machine appliqué and be sewing all the appliqué quilts you want. Enjoy yourself!

This design can be seen worked in stone over the entrance to the flower room on the front of Meadow Brook Hall, the mag-nificent Matilda Dodge Wilson estate, locat-ed on the campus of Oakland University, in Rochester Hills, Michigan. Look all around, for there is a whole world of design and inspiration just waiting to be discovered.

Plate 62.

YARDAGE

3¼ yds. pale pink stripe for background blocks
2¼ yds. gold print for borders
1 yd. maroon print for trim and binding
½ yd. terra cotta solid for flower pots
½ yd. green print for stems and leaves
⅛ yd. yellow for flower centers
¼ yd. each of four prints for flower petals –
   red, pink, brown, and black
4½ yds. for backing
81" x 96" quilt batt

CUTTING INSTRUCTIONS

Pale pink stripe:
   Cut eight 12½" background blocks
   Cut background squares on point so that
     stripe runs diagonally across blocks.

 18¼" square   9⅜" square

Figure 12.

Cut three 18¼" squares to be cut diagonally twice, (yielding four triangles per square) totaling twelve quarter square triangles used as the setting triangles. Only ten of these quarter square triangles will be used. Cut two 9⅜" squares to be cut into two triangles each for the corners. See Figure 12.

Gold print:
Cut two border strip 4" x 68½"
Cut two 4" x 58½" strip
Cut ten 12½" squares

Maroon print:
Cut nine 1" x 44" strips
Cut one 1" x 15" strip
Cut binding from the remaining fabric

Green print:
Cut 18 A's
Cut 18 AR's (leaves)
Cut 4 H's and 4 HR's
Cut one strip 1½" totaling 52" long for stems, cut pieces B and F from this strip.

Terra cotta solid cut strips:
2" x 44"
2" x 15"
3½" x 44"
3½" x 15"

Yellow:
Cut 8 D's

¼ yard prints:
Cut 24 C's for a total of 96 C's
Cut 2 G's from the brown print
Red and pink prints for border flower buds 4 G's each

SEWING INSTRUCTIONS

1. Prepare and mark background blocks for appliqué.

2. Prepare all pattern pieces for

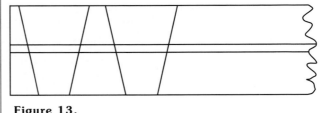

Figure 13.

appliqué as described.

3. Appliqué the Patio Pot blocks. Appliqué leaves (A & AR), in place first, then stems (B), flower petals (C), and flower center (D). The flower pot has a narrow flap of maroon print fabric separating its upper and lower parts. Construct flower pot by folding a maroon print strip 1" x 44" in half lengthwise. It will be ½" wide after folding. Insert it between the terra cotta strips that are 2½" x 44" and 3½" x 44". Have long cut edges even. Sew together with a ¼" seam. Repeat with the 15" lengths of maroon print and terra cotta. Press the seam allowance toward the narrow terra cotta strip. See Figure 13. Using the flower pot template cut out eight pots from the prepared strip of fabric. Prepare for appliqué and appliqué in place.

4. Appliqué the setting triangles in the following order: Leaves (A & AR), stems (F), and finally buds (G).

5. Appliqué the corner triangles with the two leaves H & HR.

6. The Patio Pot blocks are set on point. The quilt top will be sewn together in diagonal rows. Refer to the section on Finishing the Quilt for sewing information. Arrange the blocks according to the photograph with the gold print blocks around the outside of the quilt top.

7. There is a narrow flap of maroon print which is inserted in the seam between the quilt top and borders, as in the flower pots. Sew two 1" x 44" strips of maroon print fabric together giving a strip 1" x 87½". Fold in half lengthwise right side out. Repeat three more times giving four long narrow strips of fabric. Cut two 68½" long for the side borders. Pin to the sides of the quilt, folded edge toward the quilt's center. Sew side borders to the quilt top.

8. Cut 2 narrow strips 59" long for the end borders. Fold ¼" to the wrong side at each end of the strip. Pin to quilt ends between narrow side strips. Sew on end borders.

9. Stretch the quilt.

10. Quilt the Patio Pot blocks next to the appliqué and in lines ½" away, echoing the appliqué design. Blend the quilting lines as they get close to another block. Quilt a small flower on the lower section of the pot and a wavy line on the upper area. In the gold print blocks quilt two lines about ¼" apart. Each group of double lines will be 1" apart. Change the direction of the lines in alternate blocks. Echo quilt the buds and corner leaves. Quilt a scallop design in the outer border.

11. Bind the quilt edges with the maroon print.

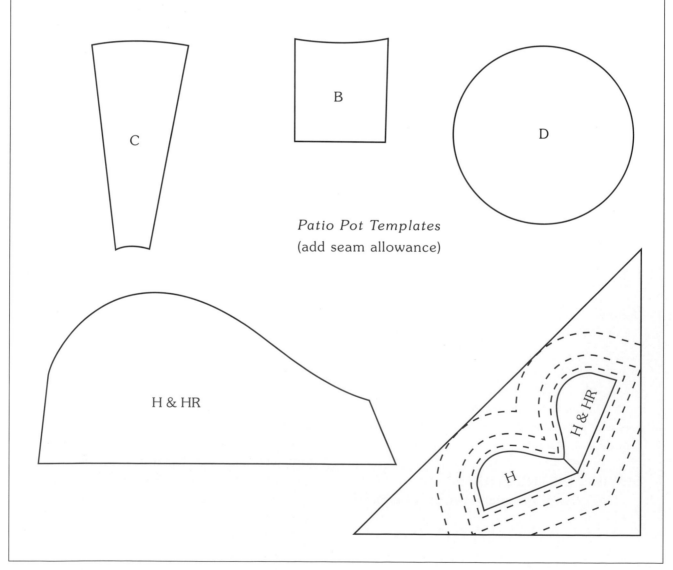

Patio Pot Templates
(add seam allowance)

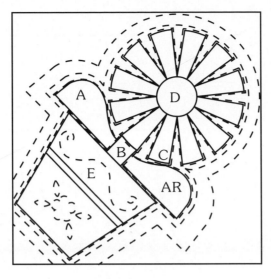

Patio Pot
Quilting Diagram

Patio Pot Template
(add seam allowance)

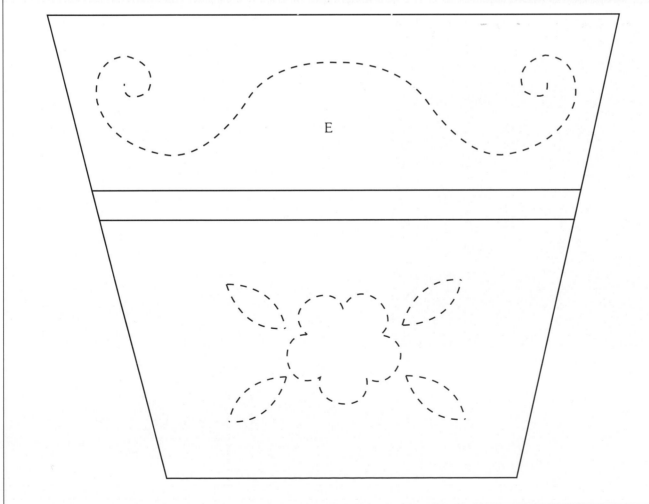

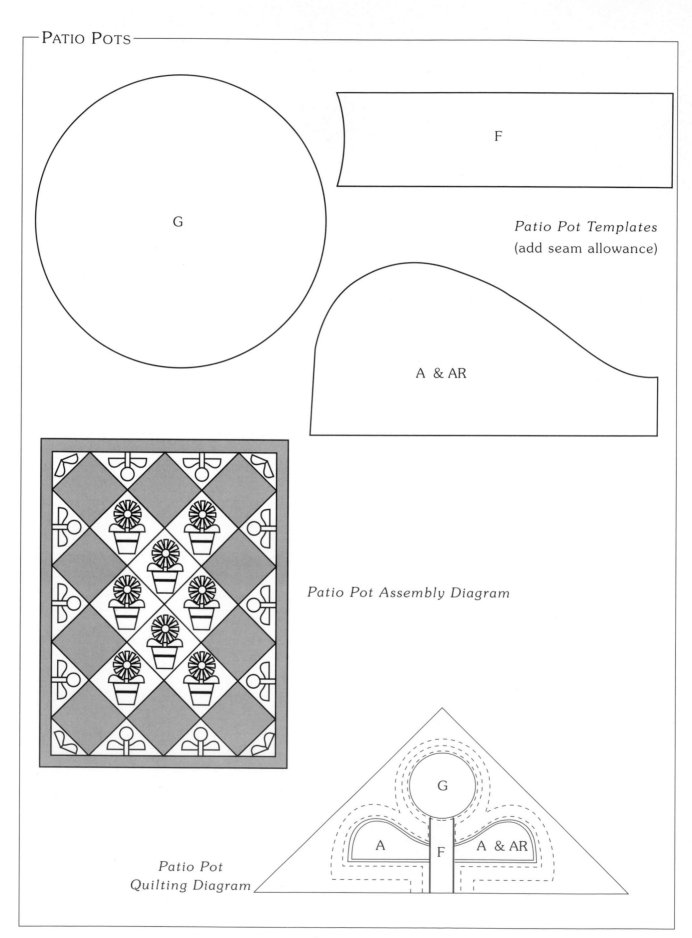

F

Patio Pot Templates
(add seam allowance)

G

A & AR

Patio Pot Assembly Diagram

*Patio Pot
Quilting Diagram*

G

A   F   A & AR

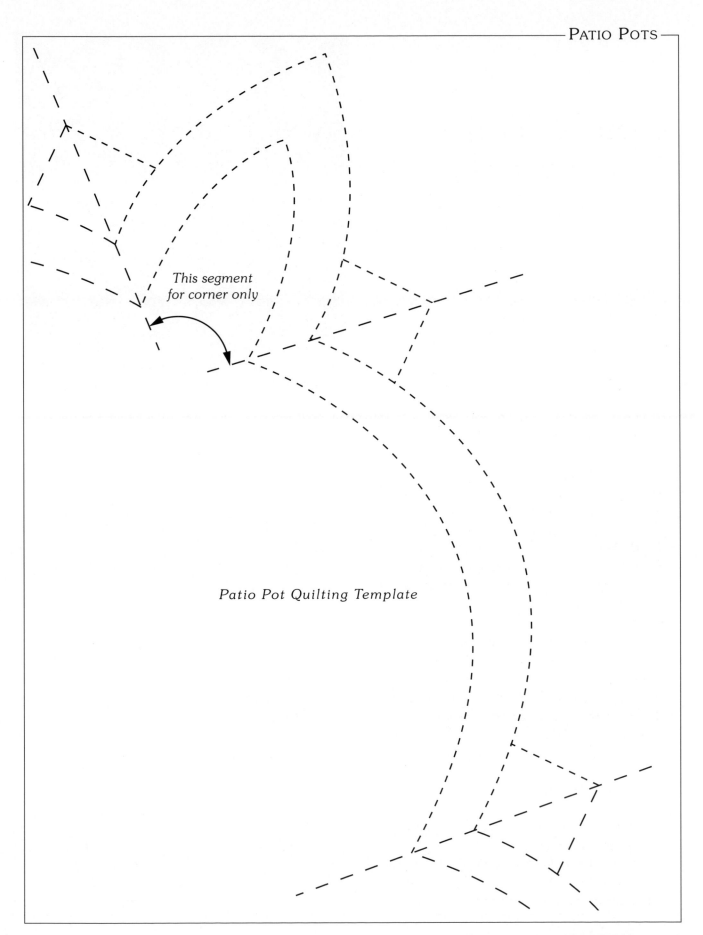

*This segment
for corner only*

Patio Pot Quilting Template

Single Tulip in a Streak of Lightning

85" x 93"

LEVEL: EASY

Color photo on page 40.

This simple Single Tulip is surrounded by the dramatic Streak of Lightning set. This c. 1880 quilt has a very contemporary look. It was machine appliquéd using the straight stitch and machine quilted.

YARDAGE

3¾ yds. muslin for background blocks
5¼ yds. green for setting triangles, leaves, and binding
1 yd. pink for flowers
5½ yds. print for quilt backing

*Your fabric should be 42" or wider. If you cut carefully there will be enough width to cut the 16¾" blocks and the 4" wide borders. If your fabric is less than 42" wide, buy an additional 2¾ yds. for the borders.

CUTTING INSTRUCTIONS

Muslin:
 Cut twenty-eight 11½" square background blocks
 Cut one 16¾" background block; cut diagonally into four triangles. See Figure 14. These will be the ends of two rows.

Green:
 Cut borders from the length of the fabric.
 Cut two strips 4" x 93½"
 Cut fourteen 16¾" squares; cut diagonally into four triangles to be used as the setting triangles for the Streak of Lightning set. See Figure 14.
 Cut six 9" squares and cut diagonally into two triangles. These are for the corners and to fill in the ends of rows 1, 3, and 5. See Figure 15.

Appliqué pieces:
 Cut 28 D's
 Cut 2 G's and 2 GR's
 Cut 28 B's
 Cut 2 E's and 2 F's
 Cut 30 A's and 30 AR's

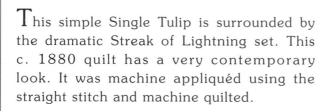

Figure 14.   16¾" square
Figure 15.   9" square

Pink:
Cut 28 C's
Cut 2 H's and 2 HR's

SEWING INSTRUCTIONS

1. Mark 28 background blocks and the muslin X triangles for placement of appliqué pieces. Prepare pieces for appliqué. Appliqué blocks in this order: A, B, C, and D. Appliqué two right half triangle blocks in this order: AR, F, HR, and GR. Appliqué two left half triangle blocks in this order: A, E, H, and G.

2. This quilt is assembled in five vertical rows. The tulip blocks are set on point and a green X triangle is sewn to opposite sides of each block, as shown in Figure 16. The row ends are filled out by the muslin Y triangles. Rows two and four end with a half appliquéd tulip block, the two left halves at the top of the quilt and the right halves at the bottom. See Figure 16. Join the vertical rows making sure the center of the setting triangle is matched to the adjacent block point.

3. Sew borders to the sides of the quilt top.

4. Layer the quilt. Quilt around each appliqué piece. Quilt a grid on the flower as shown. Quilt straight lines, parallel with the flower, 1" apart on the background blocks. Quilt the Streak of Lightning setting in straight lines 1⅜" apart following the zigzag. Quilt the side setting triangles in a V pattern with lines 1¼" apart, extending these lines out into the border. The original quilt is machine quilted.

5. Bind edges with green binding cut from the remaining green fabric.

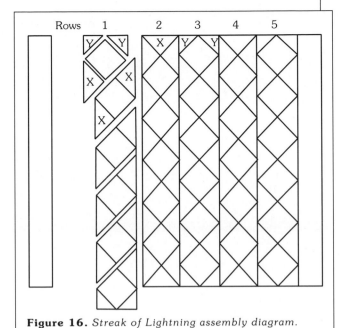

Figure 16. *Streak of Lightning assembly diagram.*

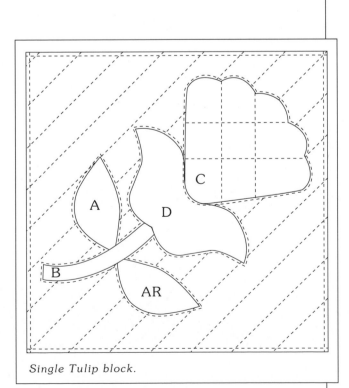

Single Tulip block.

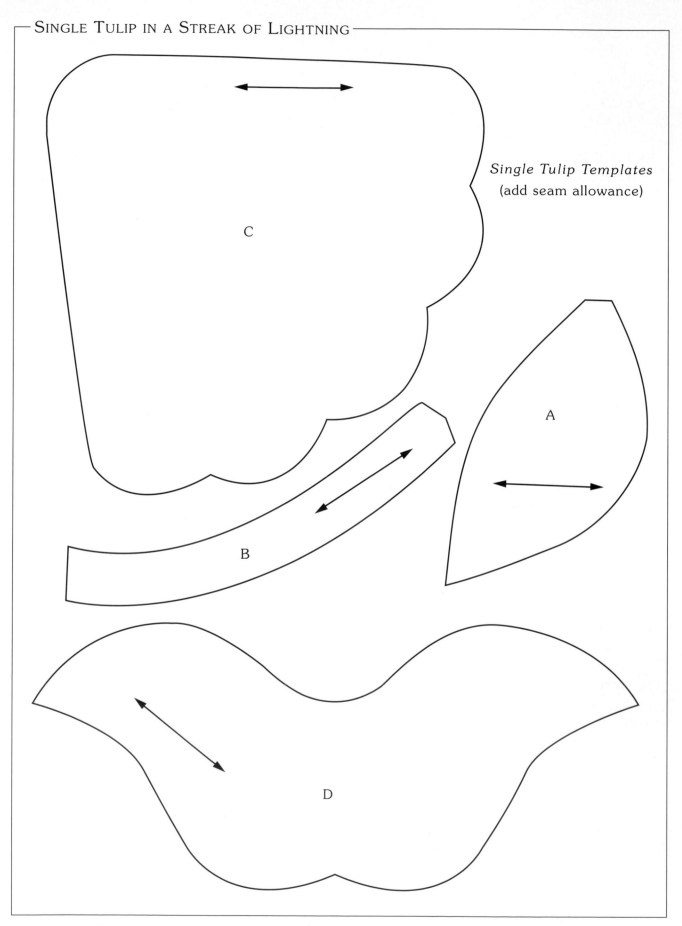

Single Tulip Templates
(add seam allowance)

C

A

B

D

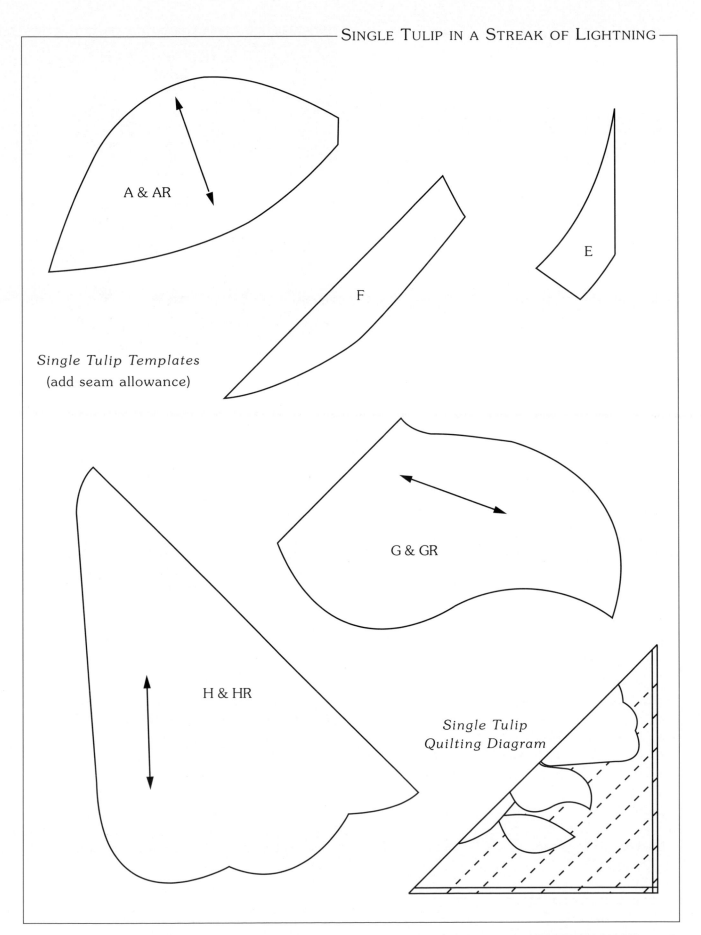

A & AR

F

E

Single Tulip Templates
(add seam allowance)

G & GR

H & HR

Single Tulip
Quilting Diagram

Reel Sampler

56½" x 56½"

LEVEL: INTERMEDIATE

Color photo on page 39.

The Reel Sampler is a showcase for some of the many ways the Reel Block can be embellished. Pictures of old album quilts showed these and many other variations. No doubt you can come up with your own version if you would like to try your hand at designing.

YARDAGE

2 yds. muslin for background
1¾ yd. medium brown print
1 yd. solid medium green
1 yd. red print
¼ yd. dark brown print
3½ yds. for backing
81" x 96" quilt batt

CUTTING INSTRUCTIONS

Background fabric – muslin:
   Cut five 15½" squares
   Cut one 22½" square
   Cut two 15⅞" squares

Medium brown print:
   Cut two 7" x 42½" strips for border
   Cut two 7" x 56½" strips for border
   Cut 12 A's
   Cut 2 B's

Medium solid green:
   Cut 68 G's
   Cut 4 I's
   Cut 4 J's and 4 JR's

   Cut 4 K's
   Cut 5 yds. 1½" wide bias for border vine
   Cut 18" x 1⅛" wide strips for stems

Red print:
   Cut 1 B
   Cut 6 E's
   Cut 8 F's
   Cut 6 H's
   Cut six 2¼" x 45" strips for Dogtooth border
   Cut 6½ yds. 2" wide bias binding

Dark brown print:
   Cut 8 A's
   Cut 2 B's
   Cut 4 D's

METHOD OF CONSTRUCTION

1. Prepare each 15½" square for appliqué. Prepare appliqué pieces for straight stitch machine appliqué. Make sure the end of piece B is neatly turned under and it covers all the raw edges of A, I, and Rose stem.

2. Appliqué each block in the following order:

   Rose – A, K, G, B, F
   Heart – A, B, E, G

Hickory Leaf – A, B, D
Leaf – A, I, B
Tulip – A, B, H, J

3. Refer to the section on Quilt Block Settings, On Point, for information on how to assemble this quilt top. Cut the muslin 22½" square into four triangles. These are used for the side setting triangles. Cut the two 15⅞" squares each into two triangles. These are the corners of the quilt top.

4. Refer to the section on Straight Stitch Machine Appliqué Borders for information on how to prepare and appliqué the borders. Make a paper pattern of the border on freezer paper, the length and width of the quilt, 6½" x 56". Use the Reel Sampler Border diagram to help position the appliqué pieces on the paper pattern. Mark placement of border appliqué pieces on the fabric borders and quilt top. Use a light table if

necessary to help in marking the design. Appliqué hearts and leaves, and tulips and leaves to the quilt top. Appliqué leaves to each border. Prepare and appliqué Dogtooth borders to the outer edge of the quilt's borders.

5. Sew borders to the quilt top. Finish appliquéing the Dogtooth borders. Appliqué the vine, then the remaining flowers and leaves.

6. Layer the quilt.

7. Quilt next to the appliqué pieces. Quilt veins in leaf and petals in flower as shown. Fill in background with tulip, heart, plume, and feather designs. Use appliqué template tulip to mark the quilting design. In the border, quilt next to the Dogtooth border. Quilt straight lines from the valley in Dogtooth border up to the vine.

8. Bind the edges with red binding.

Reel Sampler Quilt Diagram

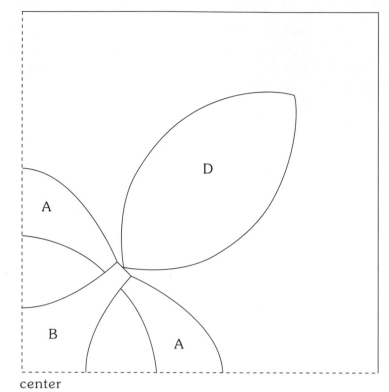

Reel Sampler Placement Guides

center

Reel and Hickory Leaf – 15" block

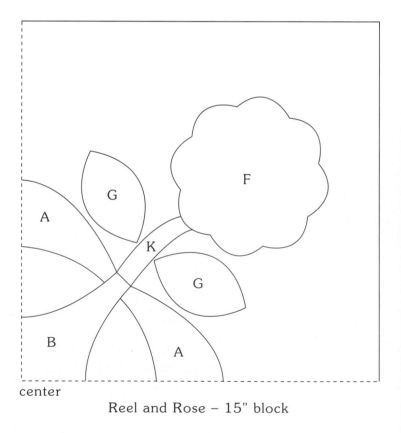

center

Reel and Rose – 15" block

Reel Sampler Placement Guides

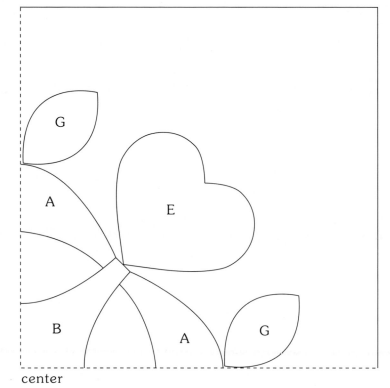

center

Reel and Heart – 15" block

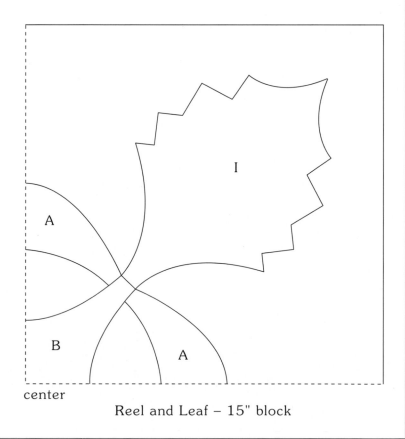

center

Reel and Leaf – 15" block

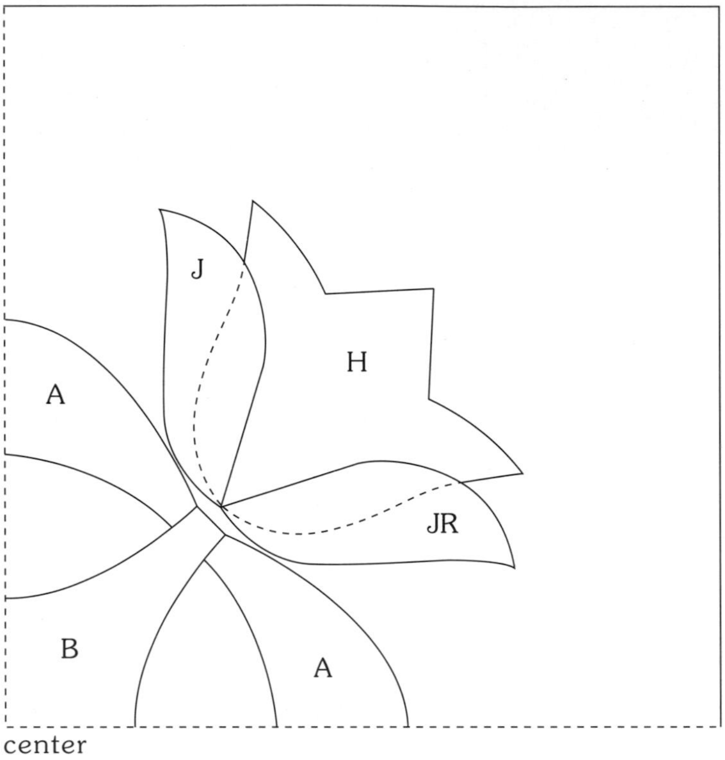

Reel Sampler Placement Guide

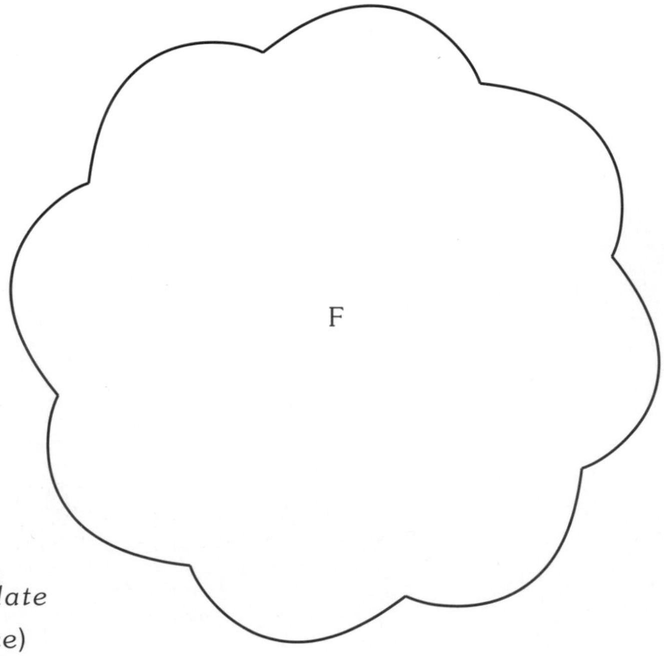

J

H

A

JR

B

A

center

Reel and Tulip – 15" block

F

Reel Sampler Template
(add seam allowance)

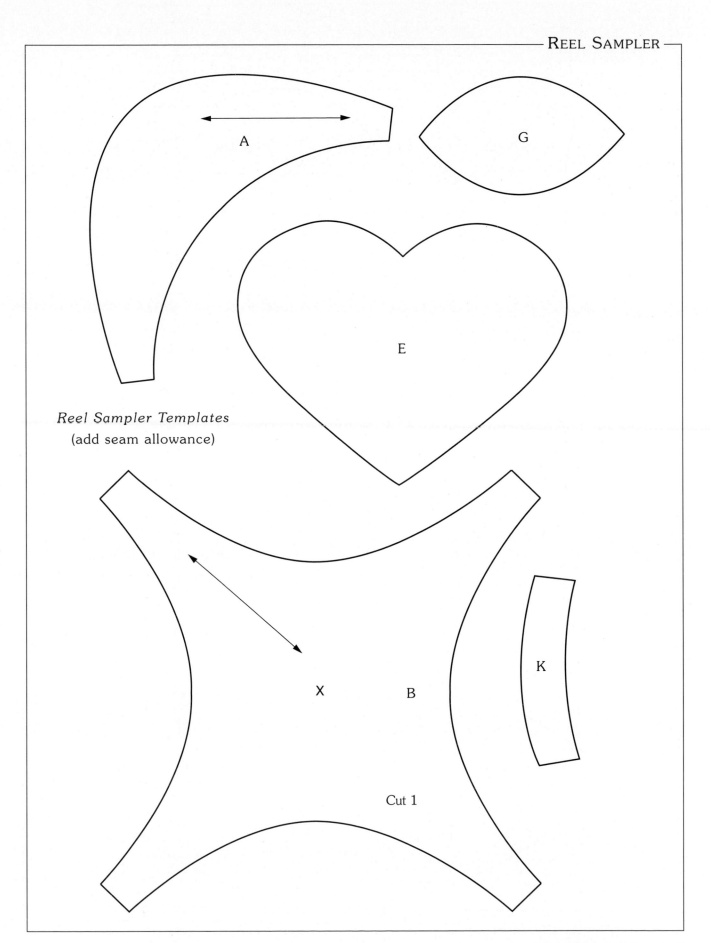

Reel Sampler Templates
(add seam allowance)

A

G

E

X   B

K

Cut 1

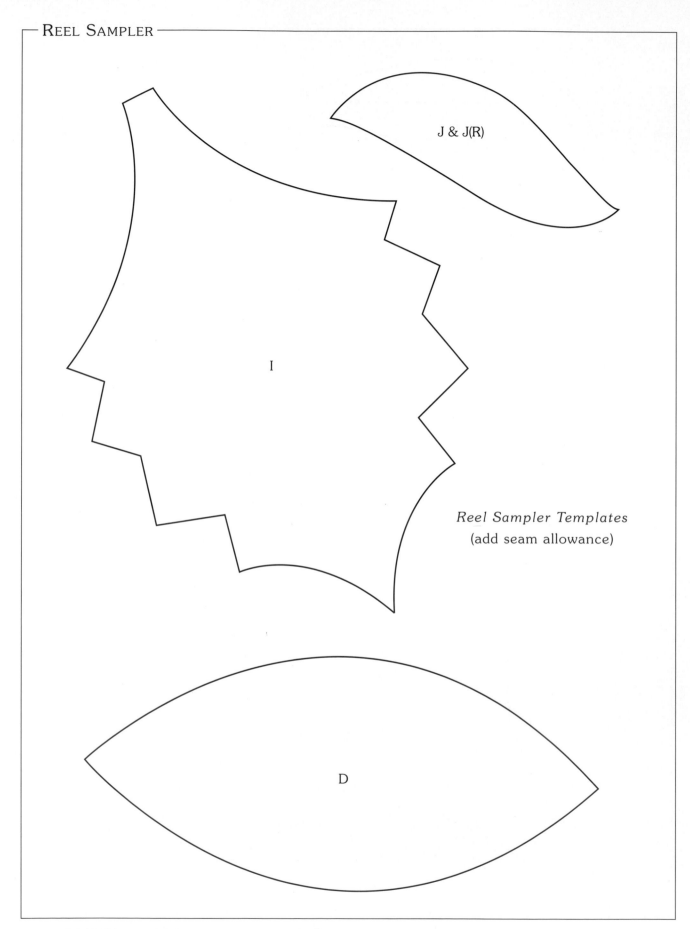

J & J(R)

I

Reel Sampler Templates
(add seam allowance)

D

Reel Sampler Quilting Templates

Reel Sampler Template
(add seam allowance)

H

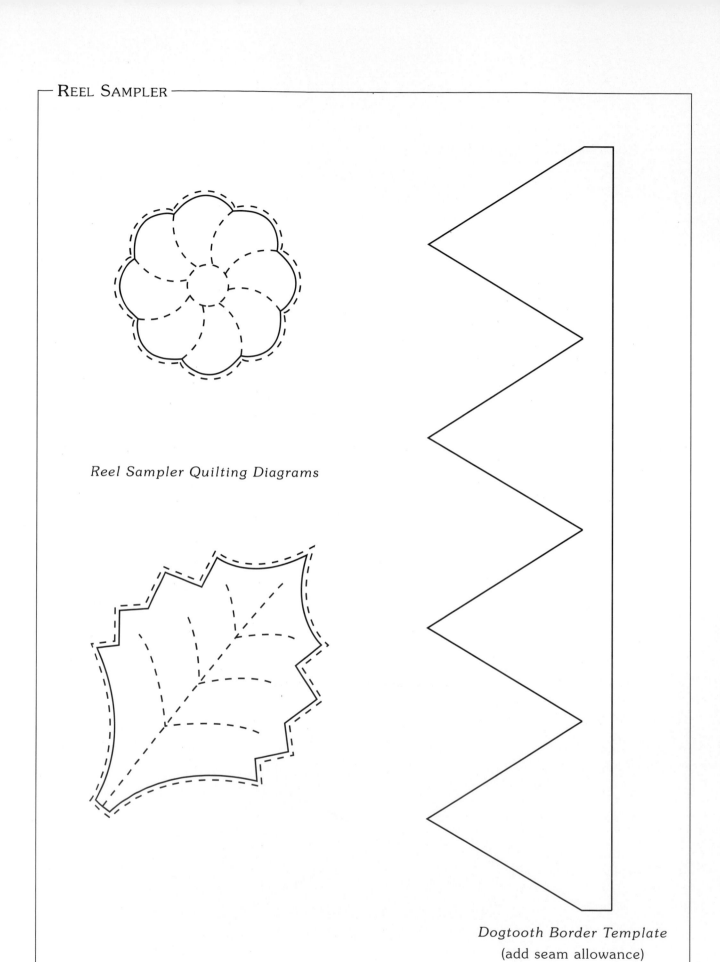

Reel Sampler Quilting Diagrams

Dogtooth Border Template
(add seam allowance)

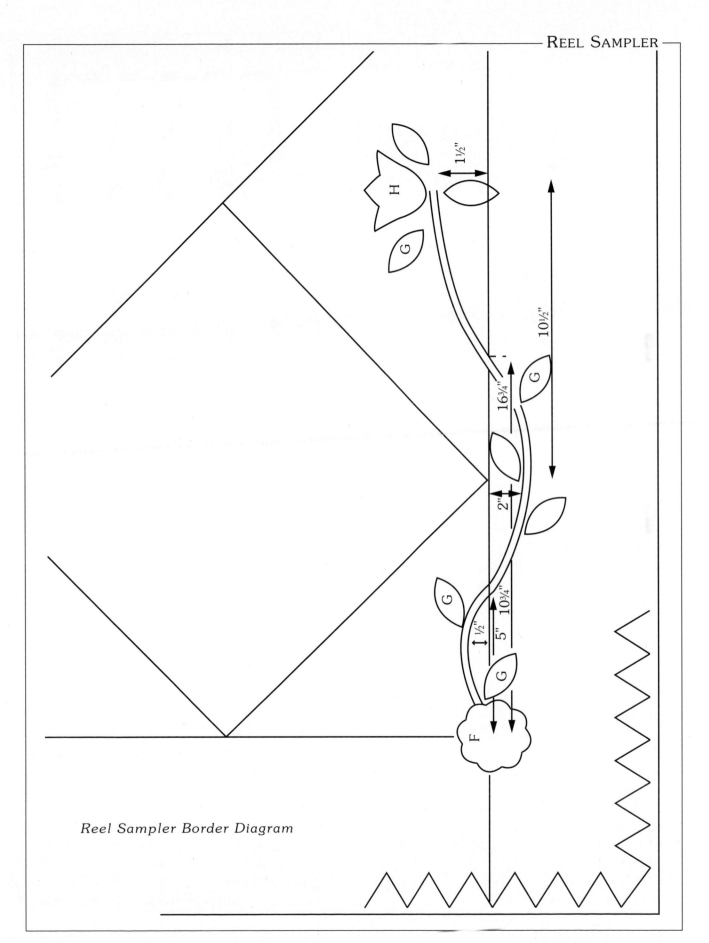

Reel Sampler Border Diagram

1930's Tulip Quilt

Twin – 62" x 82"
Wallhanging – 34" x 34"

LEVEL: EASY

Color photo on page 42.

This easy to appliqué tulip quilt from the 1930's is typically made in solid colors. Select a variety of colors or shades and tints of one color. It would also be charming with the tulips made from scraps.

YARDAGE

TWIN
Muslin 4½ yds.
Green 1½ yds.
Solids ¼ yd. each of 7 colors
Backing 5 yds.
Quilt batt 81" x 96"

WALLHANGING
Muslin 1¼ yds.
Green ½ yd.
Solids ¼ yd. of a solid. Small amount for 3
   other tulips
Backing 1 yd.
Quilt batt 36" sq.

TWIN QUILT – fifteen 8" tulip blocks set on point with a pieced inner border

CUTTING INSTRUCTIONS

Muslin:
   Cut twenty-three 8½" square background
   blocks
   Inner borders:
      Sides cut two 4½" x 56½"
   Ends cut two 3½" x 42½"
Outer borders:
   Sides cut two 8½" x 66½"
   Ends cut two 8½" x 62½"
Setting blocks:
   Cut three 13¼" squares
   Cut two 7" squares

Green fabric:
   Cut 15 leaves
   Cut 7 strips 4½" x 10" for pieced border
   Cut 2¼ yds. of 1" bias for stems
   Cut 9 yds. of 2" bias for quilt binding

Solid colors cut:
   Cut 4 tulips from each of six colors
   Cut 6 tulips from one color
   Cut 1 strip from each color 4½" x 10"

SEWING INSTRUCTIONS

1. Appliqué tulips to the 8½" blocks. Mark the background blocks for placment of appliqué pieces.

2. Prepare appliqué pieces as directed.

First appliqué stems, then leaf, and finally the two tulips. Repeat for all 15 blocks. There will be two blocks of each color and three blocks of one color.

3. Cut each of the 13¼" blocks diagonally, twice, giving four triangles per block. These are the side triangles to complete the on point set.

4. Cut the two 7" square blocks diagonally, giving two triangles per square. These four triangles are for the corners.

5. Lay out the appliqué blocks, arranging colors as you like, the plain squares, the side and corner triangles as in the diagram.

6. Sew blocks together in diagonal rows. Sew on corner blocks last. Press seam allowances away from the appliqué blocks.

7. Sew rows together. Press seam allowances down toward bottom of the top.

8. Trim so you have ¼" seam allowance around the quilt top, making sure corners are square.

9. Sew on inner side borders (4½" x 56½"). Sew on inner end borders (3½" x 42½").

10. To make the pieced inner border follow these instructions. Sew a green 4½" x 10" strip to a solid color strip of the same size. Sew along the 10" edge. Repeat for a total of seven strips. Arrange the strips of colors in a sequence you like. Sew together. Now cut into four long strips each 2½" wide by 56½" long. See Figure 17.

11. Each side pieced border will need to be 16 sections long and the end borders 11 sections long. You will need to take a section off the end border and add to the side border to get the necessary length and to keep your color sequence.

12. Because this border is made of rectangles it goes on the quilt top much like a log cabin block is made. See the diagram to help you see how they are placed. Begin sewing on a border that is even with the end of the quilt top. Sew almost to the end, stopping about 4" from the end. Begin sewing on the next consecutive border which will be even with the edge of the top. Stop 4" short as before. After sewing on the four pieced borders you can now go back and finish sewing the

2½"	Green	Red	Green	Yellow	Green	Pink	Green	Fuchsia	Green	Orange	Green	Orchid	Green	Purple
4½" x 10"														

Figure 17.

remaining few inches of each border. See Figure 18.

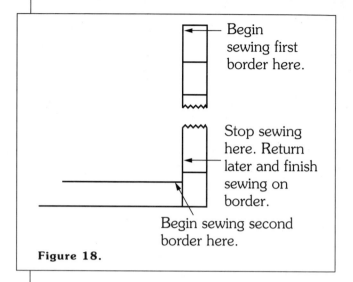

Begin sewing first border here.

Stop sewing here. Return later and finish sewing on border.

Begin sewing second border here.

Figure 18.

13. Finally sew on the wide outer side borders (8½" x 66½") and the wide end borders (8½" x 62½").

14. Your quilt top is ready for layering and quilting. Quilt around each appliqué piece. In the plain alternate blocks quilt the appliqué design reversed. Quilt the setting triangles and inner muslin border with cross hatching lines spaced 1¼" apart. Quilt a pumpkin seed design in the pieced inner border. In the wide outer muslin border quilt a vine with tulips.

15. Bind the quilt edges with green binding.

WALLHANGING – four 8" blocks set on point with an inner border

CUTTING INSTRUCTIONS
Muslin:
   Cut five 8½" square background blocks

Setting blocks:
   Cut one 13¼" square
   Cut two 7" squares for corners
Outer borders:
   Sides cut two 4½" x 26½"
   Ends cut two 4½" x 34½"

Green fabric:
   Cut 4 leaves
   Cut 20" bias 1" wide for stems
   Cut 4 yds. bias 2" wide for binding

¼ yd. of solid color:
   Cut 2 tulips
   Inner borders:
      Sides cut two 2½" x 22½"
      Ends cut two 2½" x 26½"

Small amounts of material:
   Cut 2 tulips from each of three colors.

SEWING INSTRUCTIONS
1. To appliqué tulips follow steps 1 & 2. However, you will appliqué only four blocks.

2. Follow steps 3 & 4 to cut setting triangles.

3. Follow steps 5 through 8 to assemble the quilt top.

4. Sew on inner side border of solid color fabric (2½" x 22½") then end border (2½" x 26½").

5. Sew on outer side borders (4½" x 26½") and end side borders (4½" x 34½").

6. Quilt as desired or as described for the twin quilt.

7. Bind the edges.

8½" x 66½"

4½" x56½"

2½" x 68½"

3½" x 42½"

2½" x 44½"

8½" x 62½"

1930's Tulip Quilt Diagram

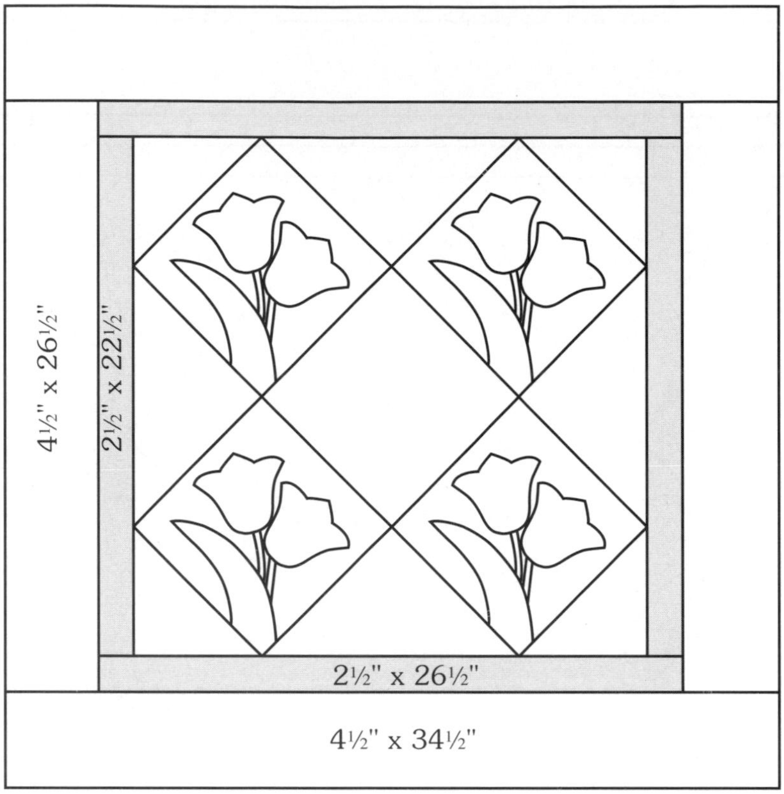
4½" x 26½"
2½" x 22½"
2½" x 26½"
4½" x 34½"

1930's Tulip Wallhanging Placement Diagram

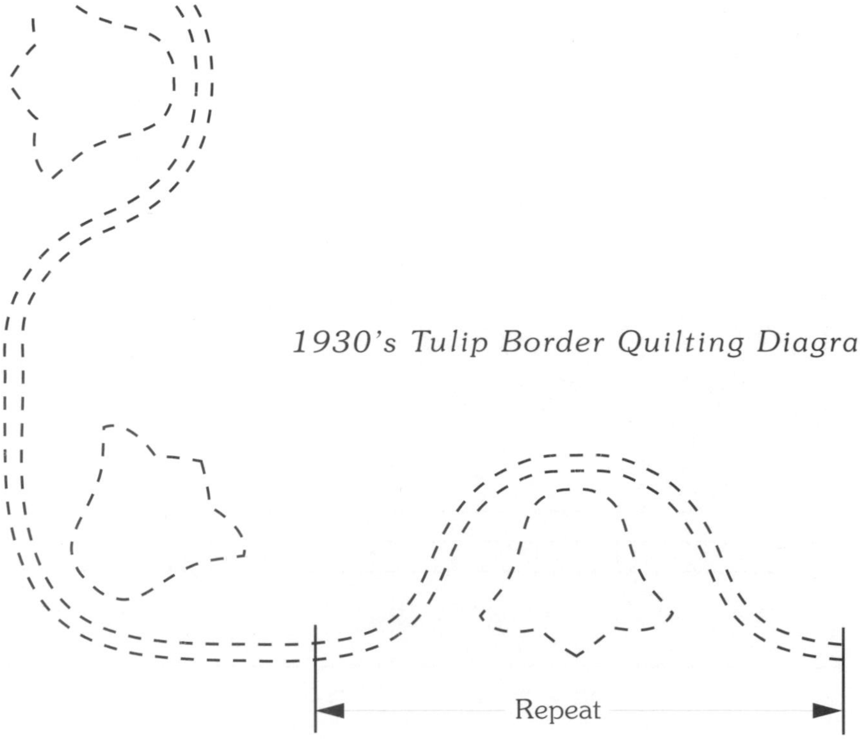
Repeat

1930's Tulip Border Quilting Diagram

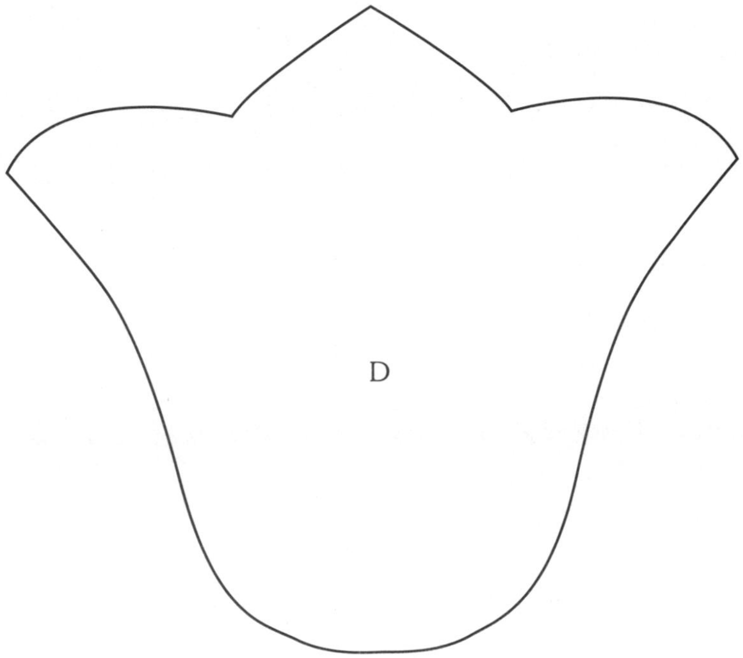

D

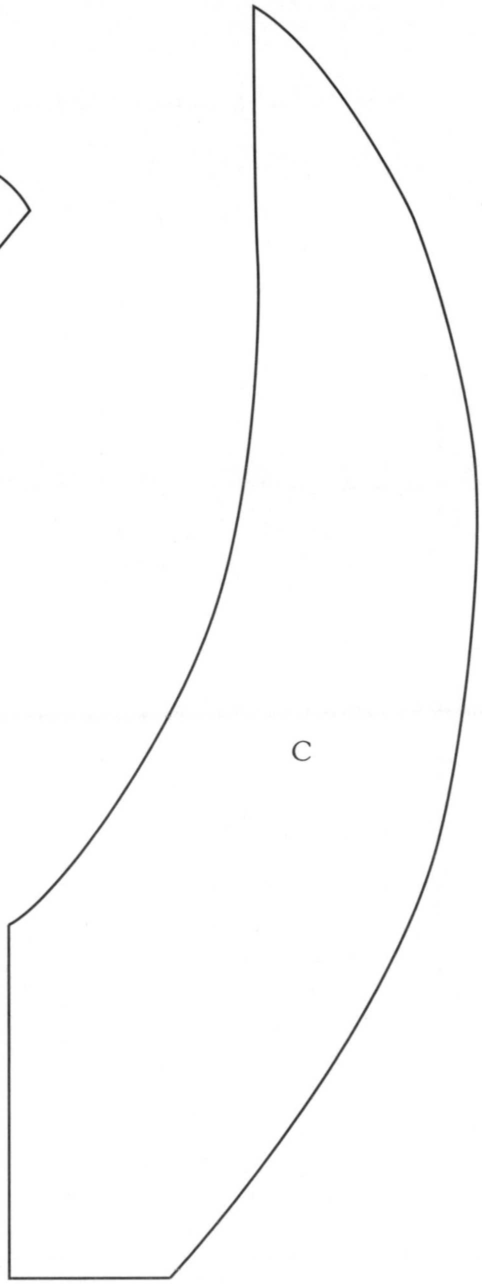

C

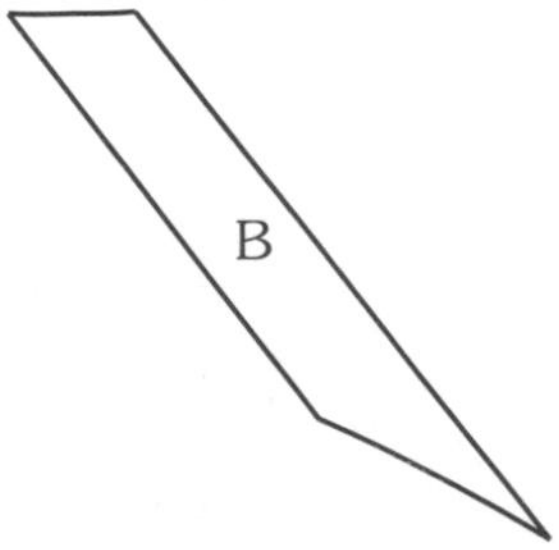

B

1930's Tulip Templates
(add seam allowance)

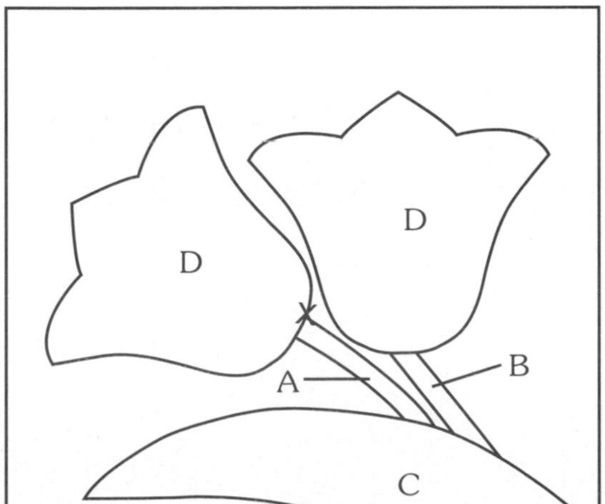

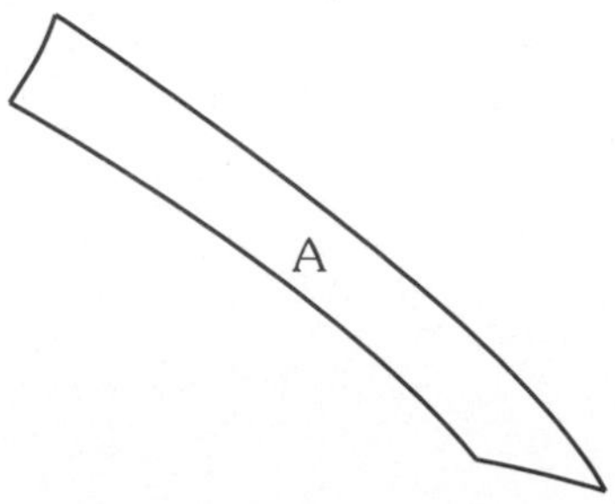

D

D

A

B

C

A

X = center of block

1930's Tulip Placement Diagram

1930's Tulip Border Quilting Template

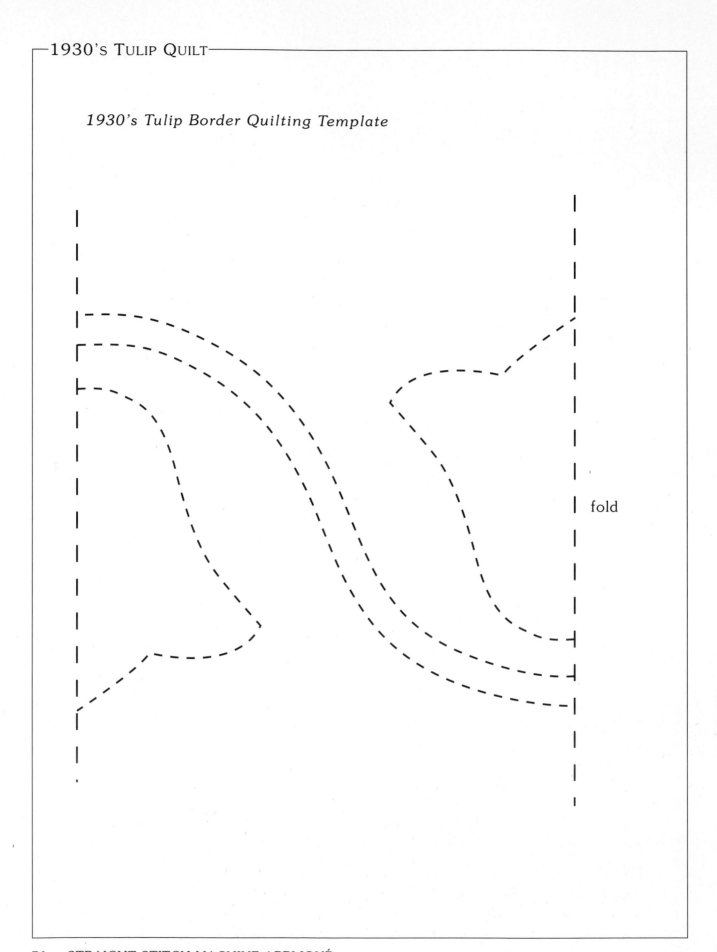

fold

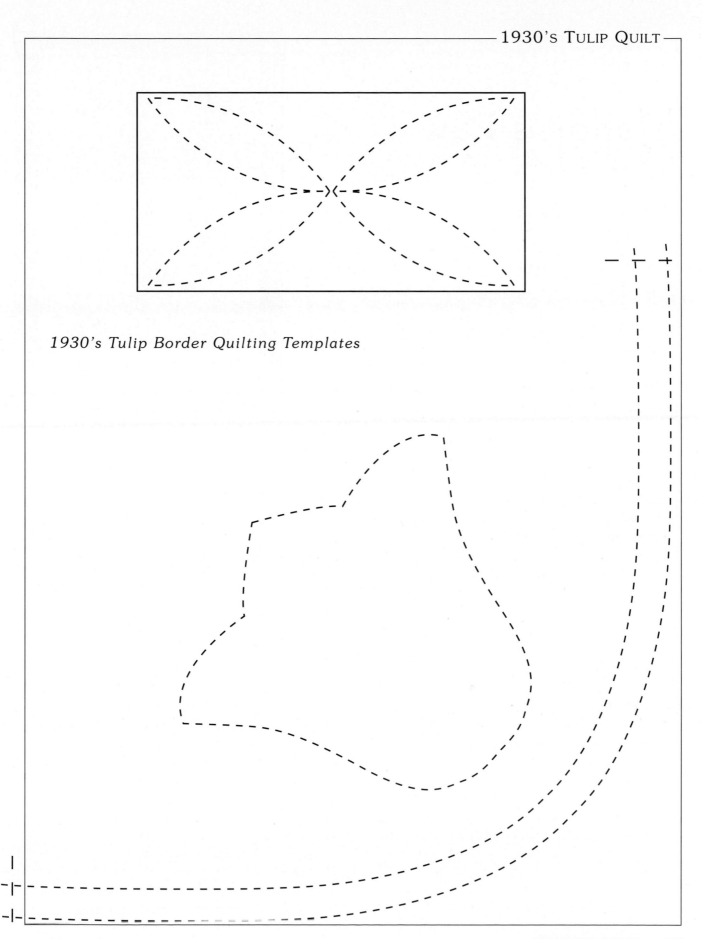

1930's Tulip Border Quilting Templates

Rabbit's Paw
34" x 48"

LEVEL: INTERMEDIATE

Color photo on page 43.

The 10" Rabbit's Paw pieced block is combined with appliquéd rabbits to create a child's crib quilt. The quilt back is also pieced. Refer to the color photograph of this quilt to check on the color placement.

YARDAGE
1 yd. beige
1½ yds. blue
1½ yds. terra cotta
¾ yd. yellow
45" x 60" crib quilt batt

CUTTING INSTRUCTIONS
Beige:
   Cut 24 A's
   Cut 28 B's
   Cut 56 C's
   Cut two 15⅜" squares
   Cut two 7⅞" squares
   Cut two 10½" squares

Terra cotta:
   Cut 56 C's
   Cut 2 rabbit appliqués
   Cut one 3⅞" x 29" strip for border
   Cut one 3⅞" x 43" strip for border
   Cut two 12¼" x 26¼" strips for backing

Blue:
   Cut 6 D's
   Cut one 3⅞" x 29" strip for border

Cut one 3⅞" x 52" strip for border
Cut one 14½" x 52" strip for backing
Cut 2¼" wide bias strips totaling 4¾ yards for binding

Yellow:
   Cut 28 B's
   Cut two 12¼" x 26¼" strip for backing

METHOD OF CONSTRUCTION
   1. Assemble the 10" Rabbit's Paw blocks. Join pieces C, a beige and terra cotta triangle to form a square. Join a yellow B to one of these triangle units. Join a beige B to a triangle unit. Sew these together. Add to each end of a beige piece A. Make two for each block. Add a beige A to each side of a blue D. Join these three strips with the blue D in the middle. Make six Rabbit's Paw blocks.
   2. Prepare rabbit shape for appliqué. Appliqué a rabbit to each of the two beige 10½" blocks.
   3. Cut each 15⅜" square into four triangles as shown in Figure 19. These will fill in the sides of the quilt. Only six of these triangles will be used in the quilt top.

4. Cut the two 7⅞" squares into two triangles as shown in Figure 20. These are the corners of the quilt top.

5. Assemble the quilt top. See assembly diagram, page 78.

6. Each of the strips you cut for the border will be cut as shown in Figure 21. Measure in ⅞" on the side at opposite ends of each border strip. Using a yard stick join the marks with a pencil line. Cut apart. Sew a blue long skinny triangle to a terra cotta triangle. Repeat so there are two long and two short border pieces.

7. Prepare four triangle units like those in the corners of the Rabbit's Paw blocks. Sew these to each end of the short borders.

8. Sew the long borders to the sides of the quilt top. Add the short borders.

9. The backing of this quilt is a piece of stripped fabric made from the colors used on the quilt top. Take a yellow and terra cotta piece of fabric, 12¼" x 26¼" place right sides together and sew together on the short side. Repeat with the other two pieces. Sew to each side of the 14½" x 52" blue strip of fabric. You will have a piece of fabric 37" x 52" to use for the backing of your quilt. See Figure 22.

10. Layer the quilt. Quilt in the ditch on the sewing machine or as desired.

11. Bind edges with blue fabric.

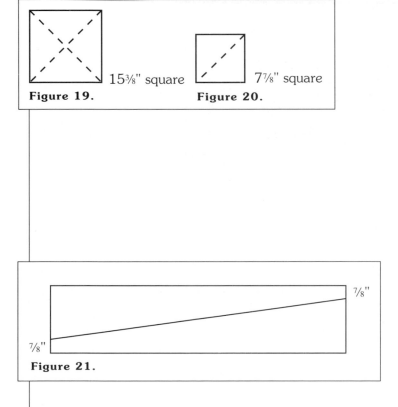

15⅜" square — **Figure 19.**

7⅞" square — **Figure 20.**

⅞"

⅞"

Figure 21.

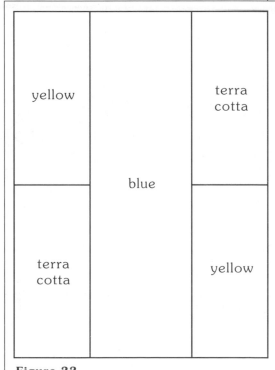

yellow

terra cotta

blue

terra cotta

yellow

Figure 22.

Rabbit's Paw Assembly Diagram

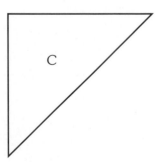

Rabbit's Paw Template
(Add seam allowance)

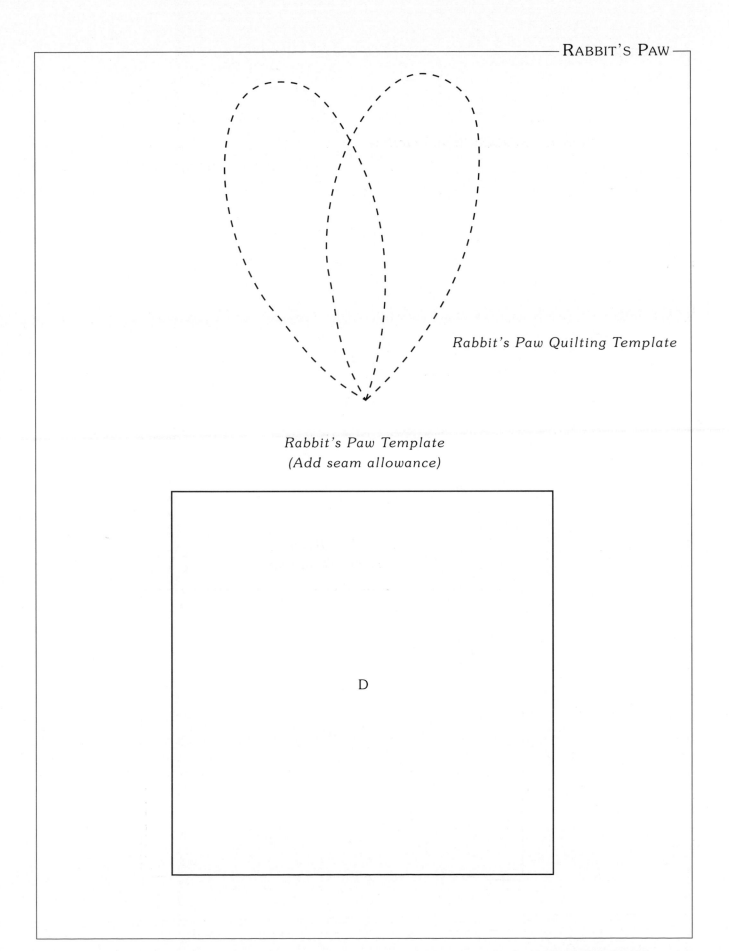

Rabbit's Paw Quilting Template

Rabbit's Paw Template
(Add seam allowance)

D

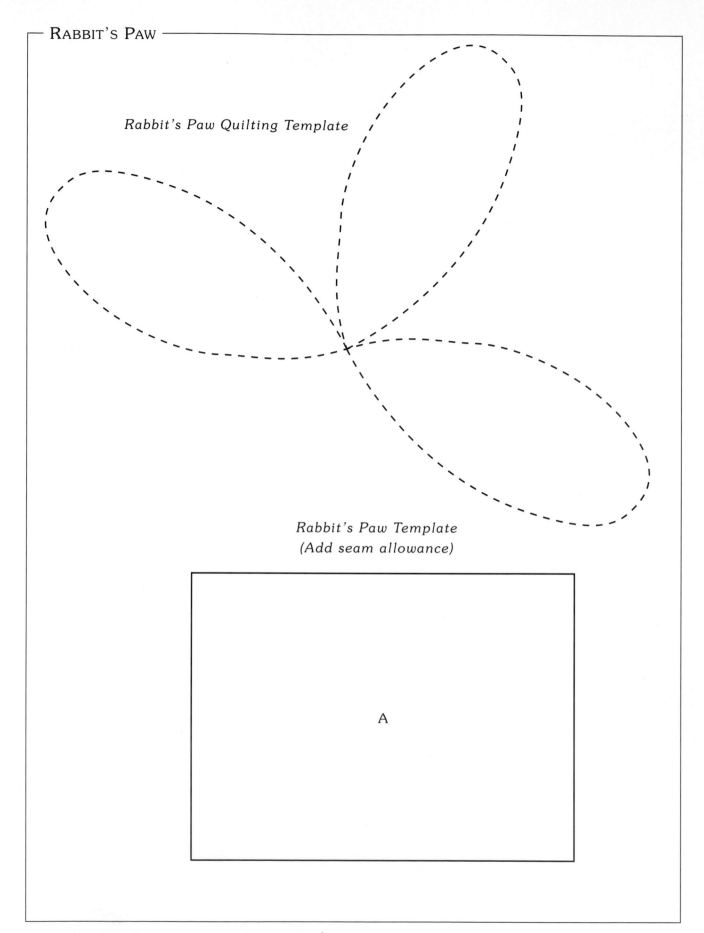

Rabbit's Paw Quilting Template

Rabbit's Paw Template
(Add seam allowance)

A

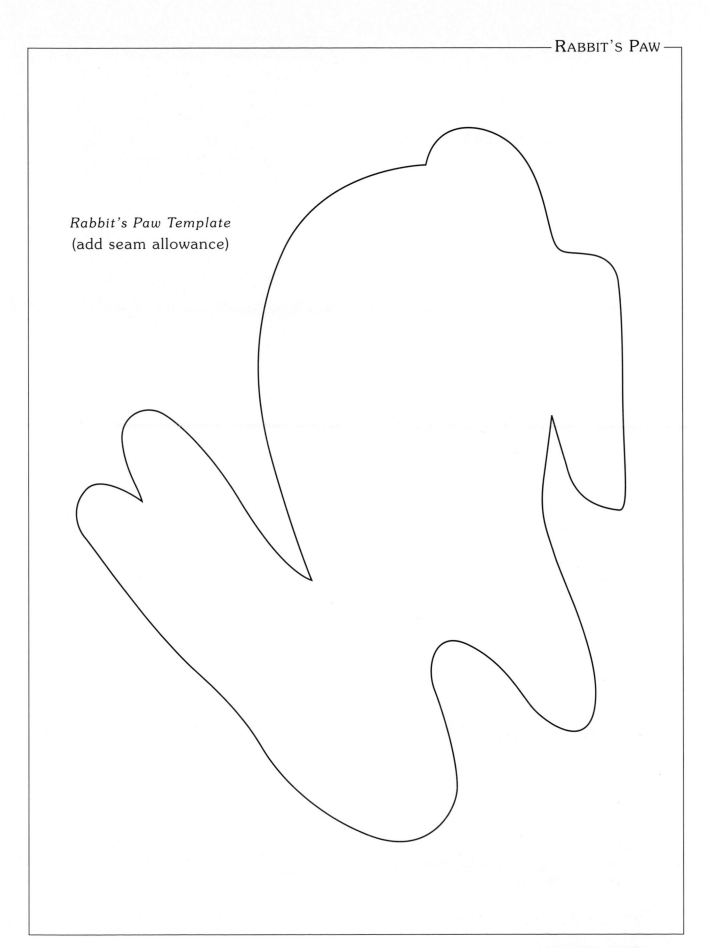

Rabbit's Paw Template
(add seam allowance)

Whig Rose
82" x 82"

LEVEL: INTERMEDIATE

Color photo on page 44.

These four large Whig Rose appliqué blocks make a dramatic quilt. The large block size means only a few blocks to appliqué and the quilt top is complete.

YARDAGE

6 yds. muslin for background blocks and borders
2½ yds. pink print for flowers, Sawtooth border, & binding
1½ yd. green for leaves and stems
½ yd. yellow for flower centers
5 yds. backing
90" x 108" quilt batt

CUTTING INSTRUCTIONS

Muslin:
   Cut four 30½" background blocks.
   Cut 2 side border strips 8½" x 66½"
   Cut 2 end border strips 8½" x 82½"
   Cut forty-two 3⅞" squares, cut into triangles for Sawtooth border

Pink:
   Cut 5 C's
   Cut 5 E's
   Cut 16 F's
   Cut 16 G's
   *Cut forty-two 3⅞" squares, cut into triangles for Sawtooth border

*The easiest way to cut the triangles for the Sawtooth border is as follows: layer pink and muslin fabric. Cut strips 3⅞" wide. Cut into 3⅞" squares. Cut into triangles.

Green:
   16 A's
   16 H's
   48 I's
   6¼ yds. bias 2¼" wide for stems

Yellow:
   Cut 21 B's
   Cut 5 D's

SEWING INSTRUCTIONS

   1. Mark four background blocks for appliqué.

   2. Prepare flower units first. Appliqué B to F yielding 16 small flower units. Appliqué 5 large flower units in this order: B to C, this unit to D, this unit to E. Prepare stems for appliqué.

   3. Appliqué the blocks in the following order: A, bud and flower stems, G, H, small flower units, large flower unit, and I.

   4. Join the four 30" blocks. Where the seams meet, center and appliqué one large flower unit.

   5. Pick up and sew together a pink and

muslin triangle. Repeat until there are 84 pink and muslin squares for the Sawtooth border. Arrange as shown in photograph. Sew twenty squares together reversing direction of the pink triangles in the middle of the border. Sew four strips, two will be the side borders and two the end borders. The pink triangles will be next to the appliqué blocks. To each side of the end borders sew another square with the pink triangle in the outer corner. Sew the side Sawtooth borders to the quilt top, then the end Sawtooth borders.

6. Sew the muslin borders to the quilt top. Sew on the side borders, 8½" x 66½". Last sew on the end borders, 8½" x 82½".

7. Layer the quilt.

8. Quilt around each appliqué piece ¼" away. Quilt the background in lines 1" apart radiating out from the center to the cable design in the outer muslin borders.

9. Cut 9¼ yards 2" wide bias from the remaining pink fabric. Bind with pink binding.

Whig Rose Templates
(add seam allowance)

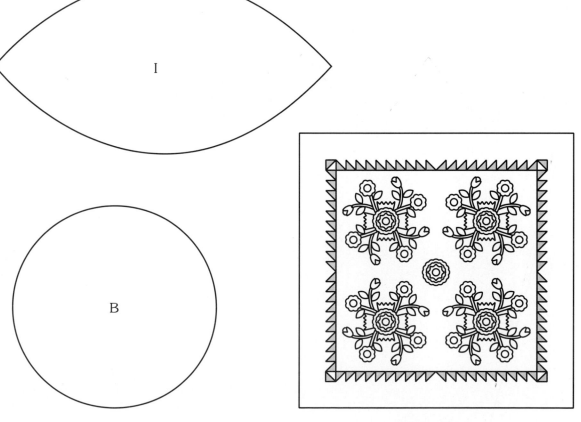

Whig Rose
Assembly Diagram

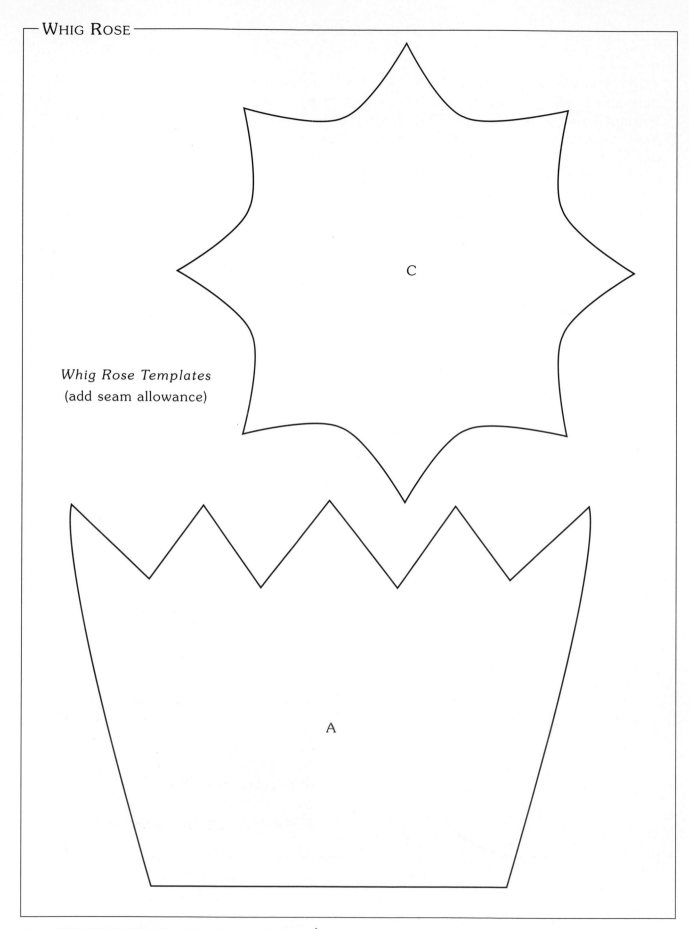

Whig Rose Templates
(add seam allowance)

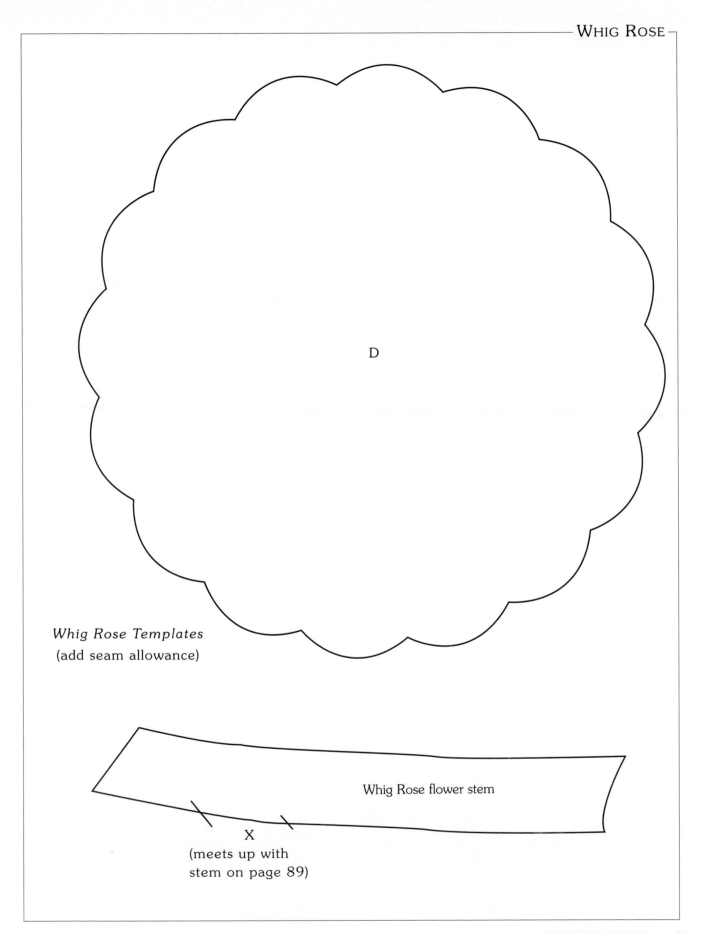

D

Whig Rose Templates
(add seam allowance)

Whig Rose flower stem

X
(meets up with
stem on page 89)

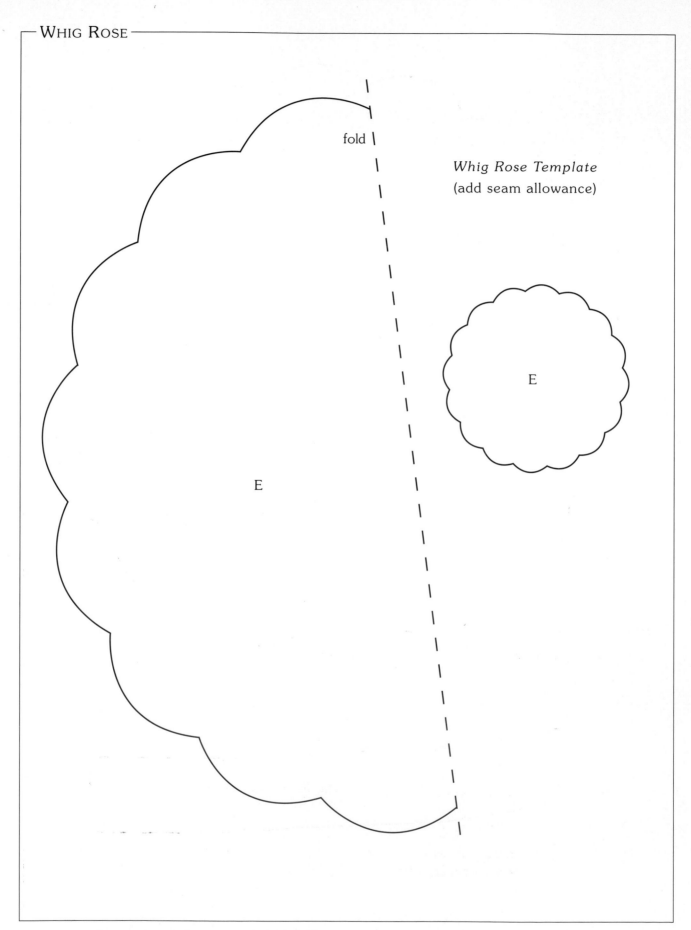

fold

Whig Rose Template
(add seam allowance)

E

E

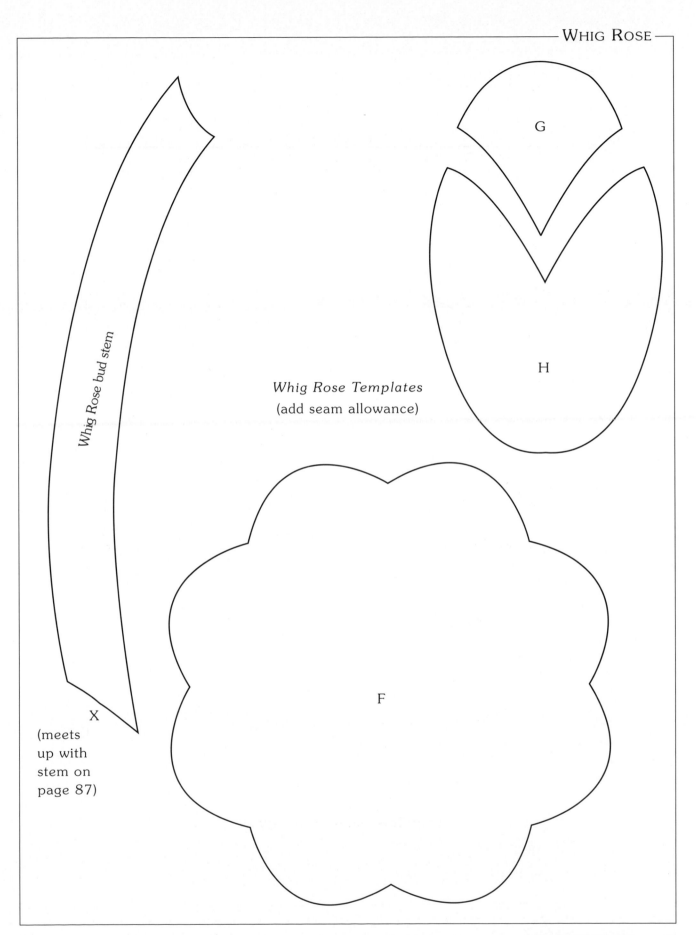

Whig Rose bud stem

Whig Rose Templates
(add seam allowance)

G

H

F

X

(meets
up with
stem on
page 87)

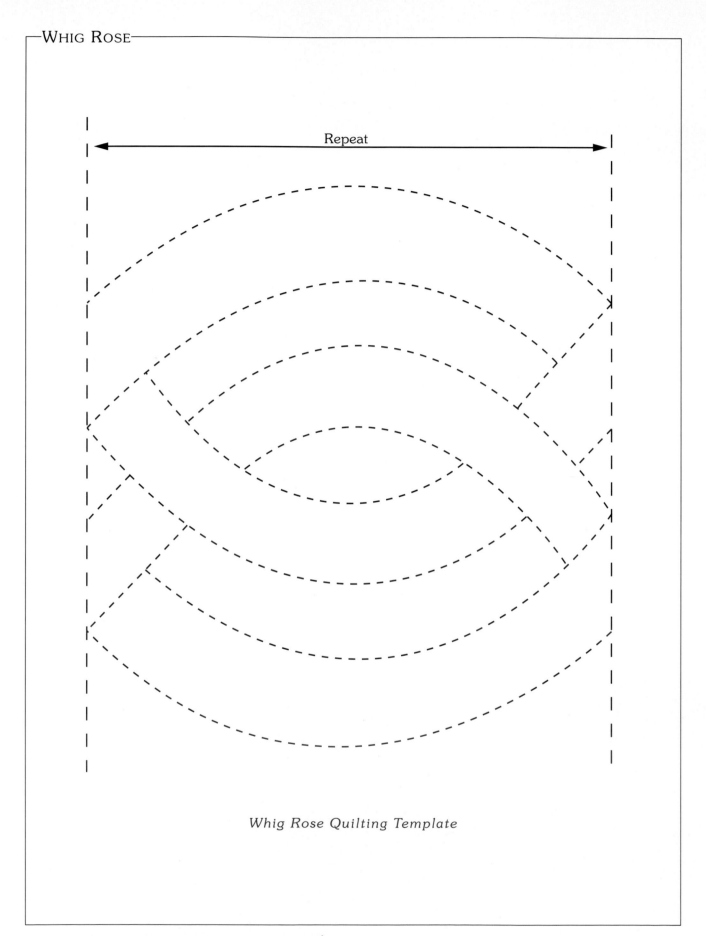

Repeat

Whig Rose Quilting Template

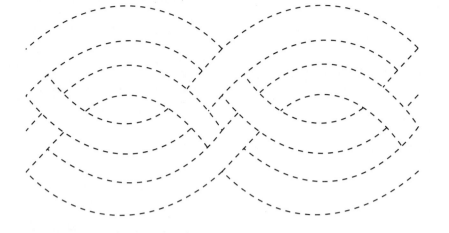

Whig Rose Quilting Diagrams

Floral Medallion
91" x 103"

LEVEL: INTERMEDIATE

Color photo on page 45.

An assortment of beautiful flowers scattered around an oval wreath creates a striking medallion style quilt. The medallion is framed by a scalloped border and quilted vining feathers. The center medallion fits a twin bed and adjusts to full or queen size by adding different width side panels. The quilt length allows for tucking under a pillow with quilted vining feathers laying across the pillow top. Yardage and instructions are given for a queen size quilt, with variations for the other sizes.

YARDAGE

6 yds. white for background
3 yds. gold print for borders
¼ yd. gold solid
½ yd. yellow solid
⅛ yd. light medium green print
½ yd. medium green solid
⅛ yd. dark green print
⅛ yd. light medium pink print
½ yd. medium pink print
1 yd. medium green solid for quilt binding
9 yds. white for quilt back
90" x 108" quilt batt, all sizes

CUTTING INSTRUCTIONS

QUEEN SIZE QUILT

White background fabric:
    Cut 1 center panel 37½" x 83½"
    Cut 1 end panel 10¼" x 37½"

Cut 2 side panels 22¼" x 93½"

Special cutting instructions for side panels for twin or full size quilts.
    TWIN – Cut 2 side panels 10¼" x 93½"
    FULL – Cut 2 side panels 19" x 93½"

Gold print border fabric:
    Cut 2 side borders 8" x 83½"
    Cut 1 end border 8" x 61½"
    Cut 1 top border 4½" x 91½"
    Cut 2 corner squares 15½" x 15½"

Appliqué Pieces
Yellow solid:
    Cut 5 B's
    Cut 1 D
    Cut 6 E's
    Cut 17 F's
    Cut 14 O's
    Cut 10 P's

Medium pink print:
    Cut 5 B's
    Cut 17 G's
    Cut 2 L's

Light medium pink print:
  Cut 1 C

Gold print:
  Cut 1 A
  Cut 2 C's

Gold solid:
  Cut 4 C's
  Cut 4 J's

Medium green solid:
  Cut 13 H's
  Cut 16 M's
  Cut 14 N's
  Cut 10 Q's
  Cut 3½ yds. of 1½" wide bias for stems and wreath

Light medium green print:
  Cut 4 I's
  Cut 4 H's

center panel

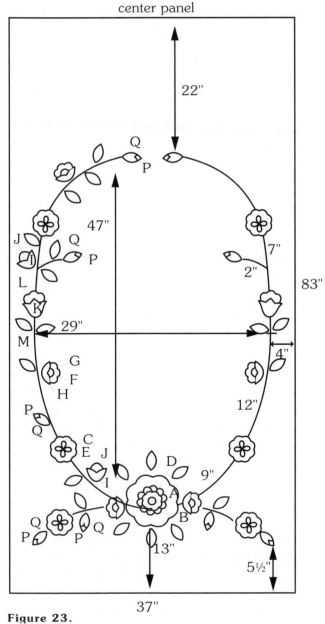

Figure 23.

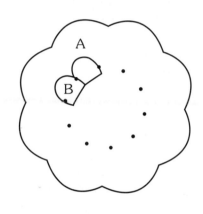

Figure 24.

Dark green print:
  Cut 2 K's
  Cut 14 M's

METHOD OF CONSTRUCTION

Prepare appliqué pieces for straight stitch machine appliqué. Refer to photograph and drawing to help with color and placement of flowers and leaves.

CENTER PANEL

1. Mark the placement lines for the oval wreath and flowers on the center panel. Refer to Figure 23 for measurements. Prepare bias and appliqué in place on the center panel. Appliqué stems branching into the wreath center first so its raw edges will be underneath the main wreath.

2. Prepare main center flower unit as follows: Appliqué B pieces, alternating colors, to A. See Figure 24. Use notches on B pattern piece to help with spacing. Appliqué D to C. Appliqué this unit to the petal unit. Appliqué the entire flower unit to the center panel.

3. Prepare and appliqué E to C. Appliqué the flower units to the center panel.

4. Prepare and appliqué L and K to center panel.

5. Prepare and appliqué P and Q in place, also J and I.

6. Appliqué F to G. Appliqué this unit to center panel, add H.

7. Prepare and appliqué M in place. The center panel is now completed.

BORDERS

Before adding the borders reread the section on appliqué borders in the section, Finishing the Quilt.

1. Using the template, mark and cut the scallops on the upper edge of the end gold print border. See Figure 25. There are six scallops. A point should be at the center of the gold print border. Prepare for appliqué, match centers, and add to the white end border. The gold print border is longer than the white border and the extra fabric will be appliquéd to the side panels when they are added. For now, fold up the extra fabric and pin. Mark placement and appliqué in place the center flower on the end white border. Appliqué a bud on either side of the center flower. These are located above the points of the scallops.

2. Center and sew the end white border unit to the bottom edge of the center panel.

3. Mark and cut the scallops on the upper edge of the gold print side borders. See Figure 26. The first scallop should begin ¼" from the left end of one border and right end of the other border. This edge will be joined to the corner pieces. Prepare and appliqué to the white side panels, beginning to sew at the opposite end from which you marked the scallops. The white side border is longer than the gold print border. The corner unit will fill in the gap. Leave the corner end of the gold print border free about 3" when sewing. Mark the placement of and appliqué in place alternating flowers and buds, beginning and ending with a bud.

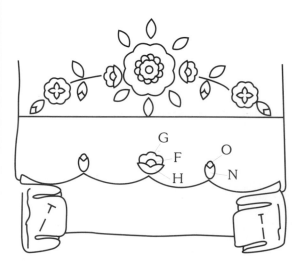

Figure 25.

4. Sew side border units to the side of the center panel.

5. Cut scallop on the gold print corners. Prepare for appliqué. Sew corner sides to ends of the side and end gold print borders. Appliqué in place the remaining scallops. Please note that on the full and twin size quilts it may be necessary to change the corner curve so it will smoothly flow around the corner.

6. Mark placement of remaining buds and flowers. Fold quilt top up as small as possible, but still giving you access to the area to be appliquéd. Appliqué in place the remaining buds and flowers on the border.

7. Trim away the excess white fabric on the wrong side under the gold print border. Round the bottom corners of the gold print border.

8. Sew the narrow gold print border to the top of the quilt. The top is complete and now ready to be marked for quilting.

9. Mark oval feathered wreath in center of the appliquéd flowers. See Figure 27. One inch cross hatching is marked in the center of the feathered wreath. Mark a feathered vine on each side of the center panel, having the center of the flower be 6½" from the side seam of the center panel. Across the quilt top mark the same design 12" from the outer edge. Mark corner designs 5½" from corner scallop. Mark background diagonal quilting lines 1½" apart from center out to the scalloped borders. Using the scallop template mark three scallop quilting lines on the gold print border, spacing the lines 1¼" apart at the center. Quilt around each appliquéd flower and leaf and vine.

10. After quilting, cut scallops on the border. Baste the raw edges together and bind with bias binding, cut 2" wide. See Finishing the Edges with Binding for detailed information.

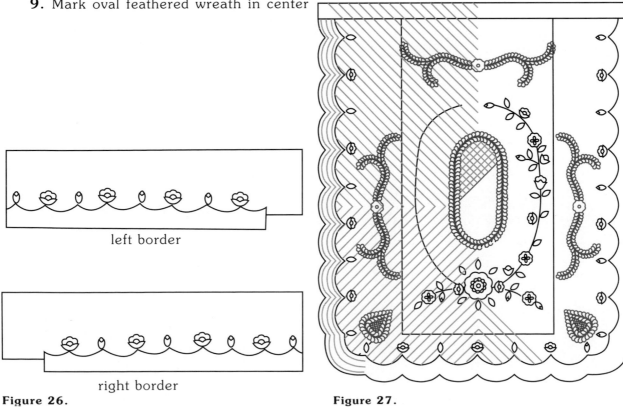

left border

right border

Figure 26.

Figure 27.

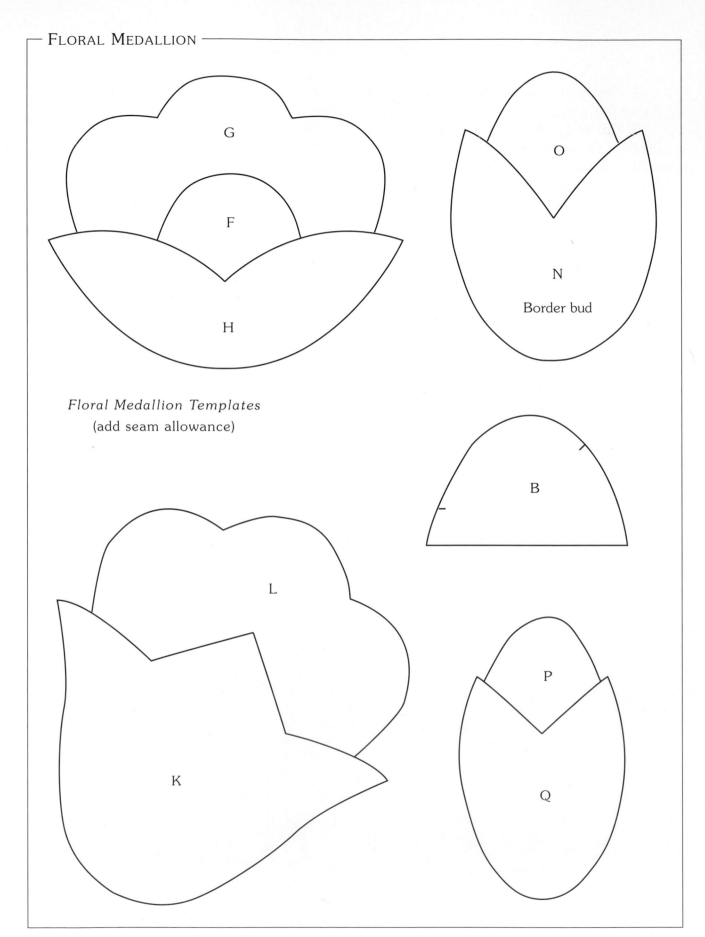

G

F

H

O

N

Border bud

Floral Medallion Templates
(add seam allowance)

B

L

K

P

Q

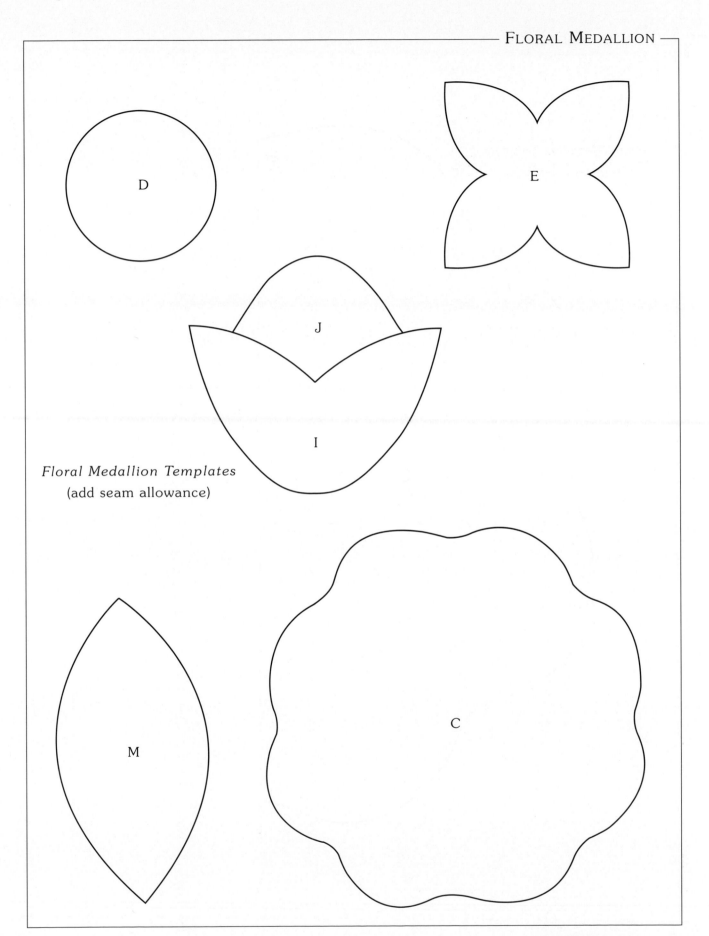

Floral Medallion Templates
(add seam allowance)

Floral Medallion Template
(add seam allowance)

fold

A

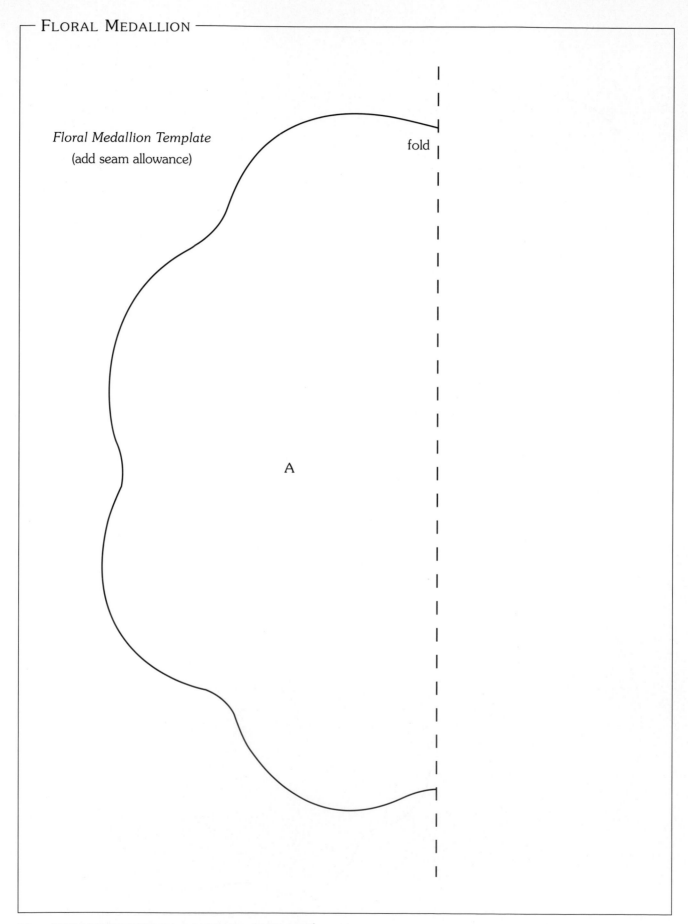

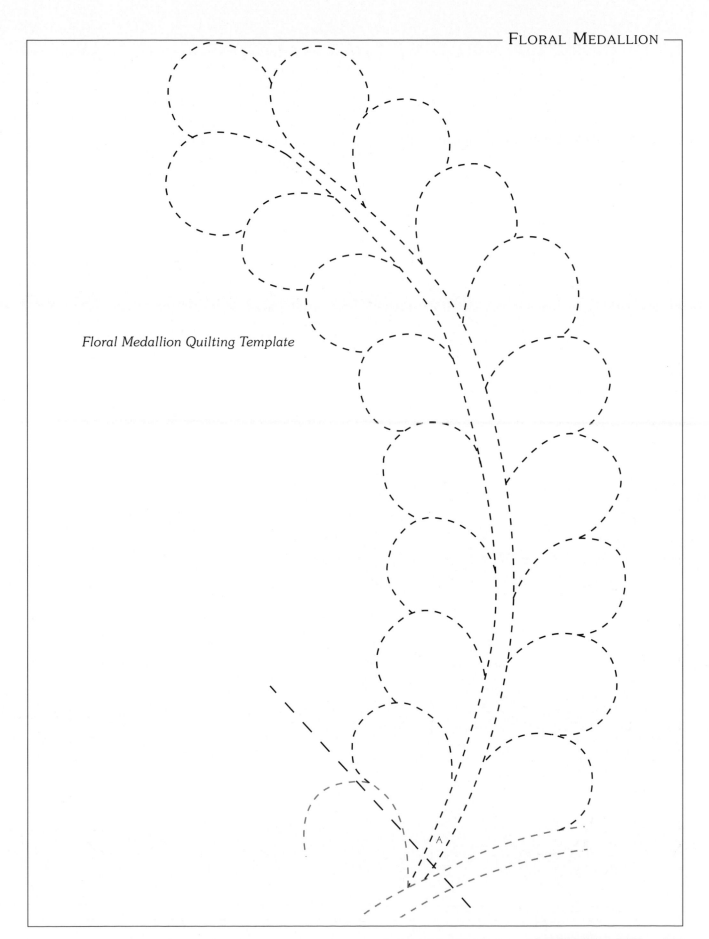

Floral Medallion Quilting Template

Floral Medallion Quilting Template

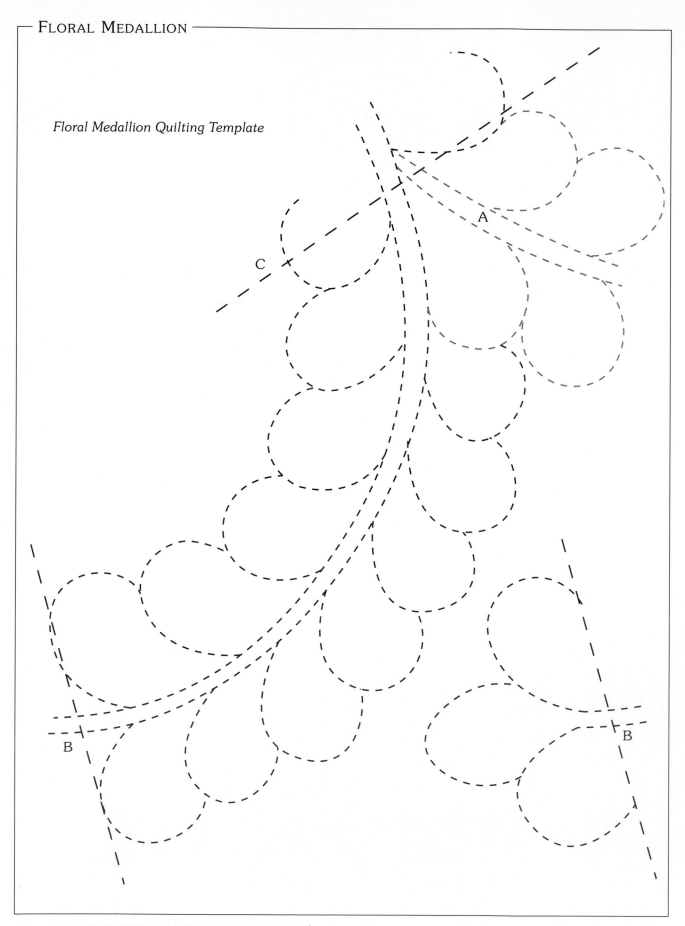

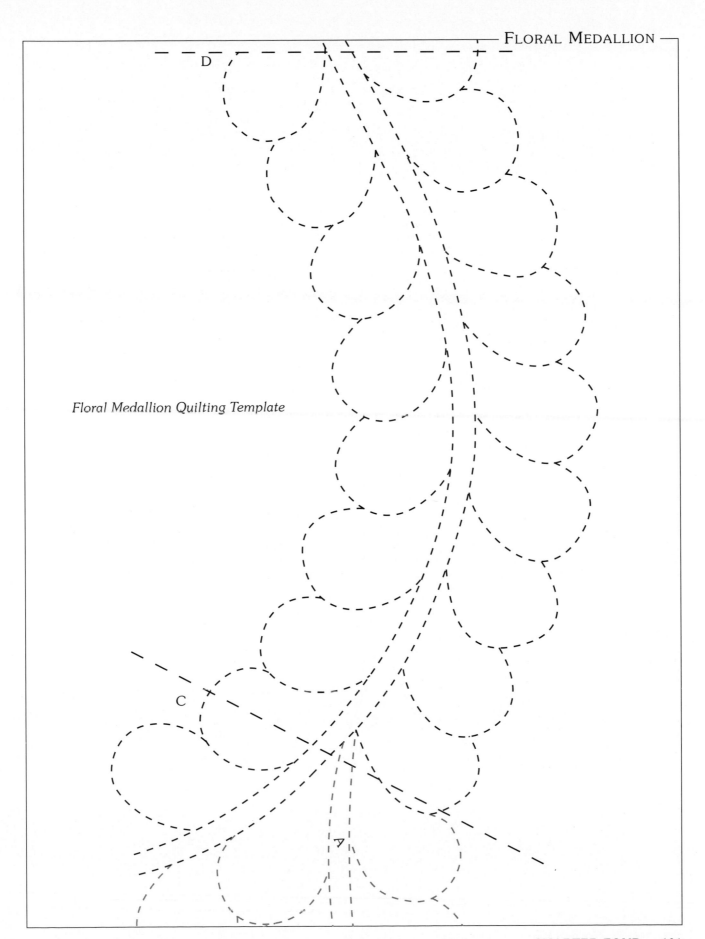

Floral Medallion Quilting Template

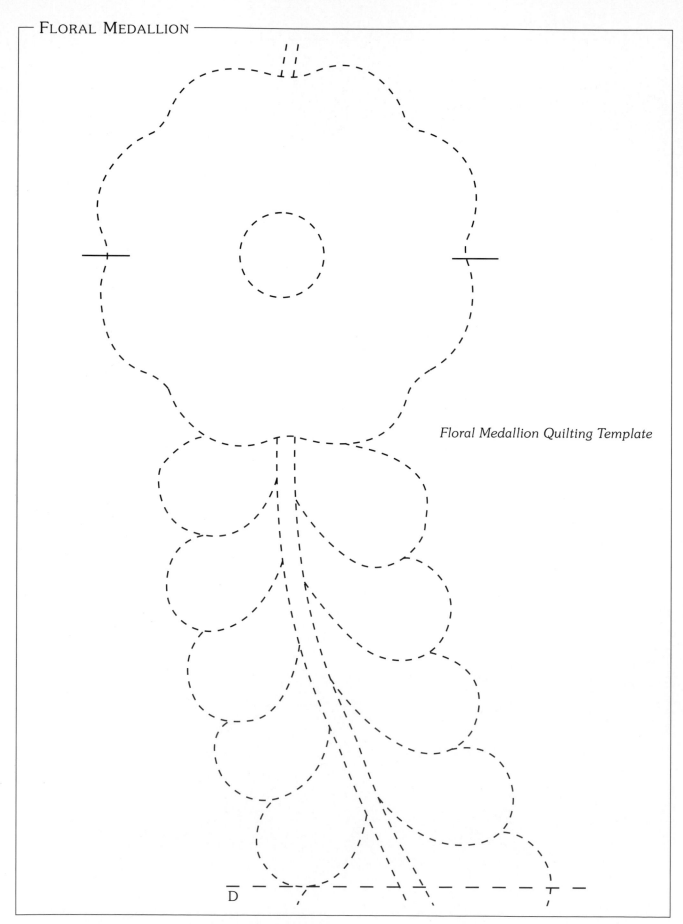

Floral Medallion Quilting Template

D

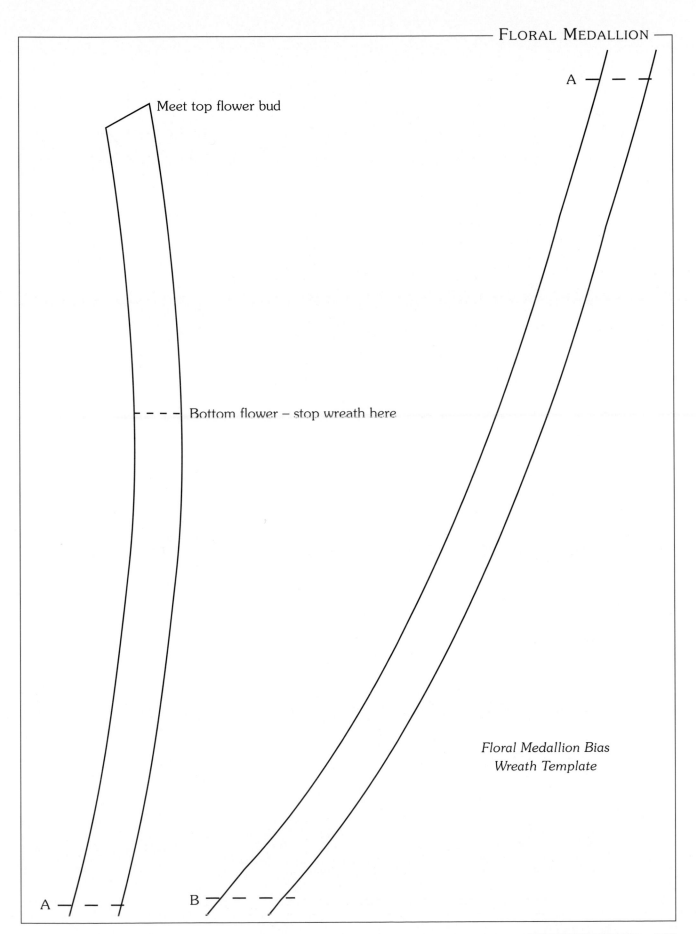

A

Meet top flower bud

- - - Bottom flower – stop wreath here

*Floral Medallion Bias
Wreath Template*

A - - -   B - - -

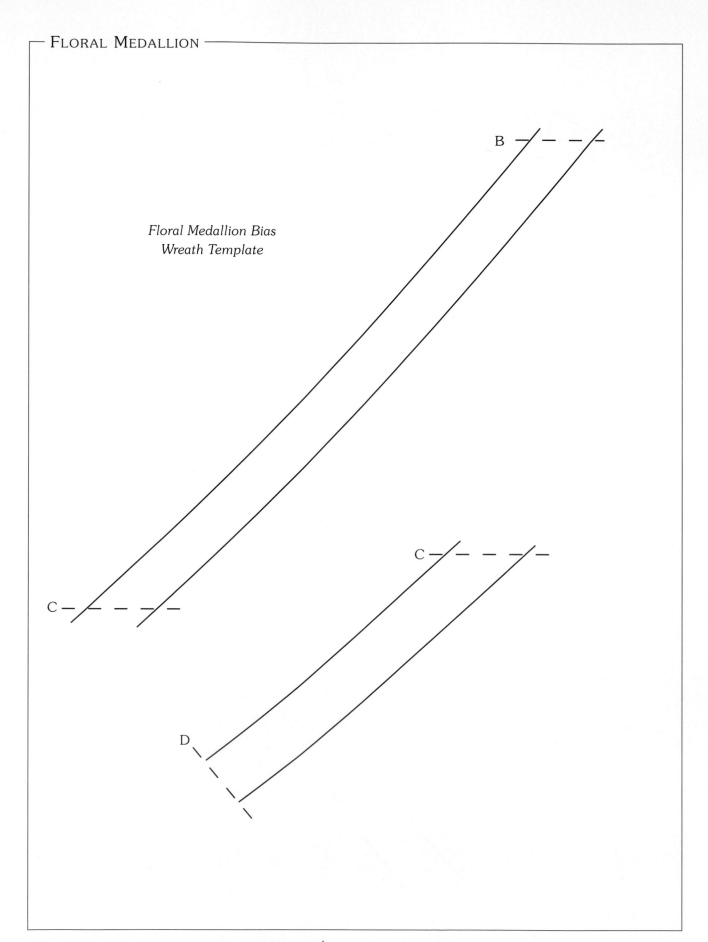

*Floral Medallion Bias
Wreath Template*

B

C

C

D

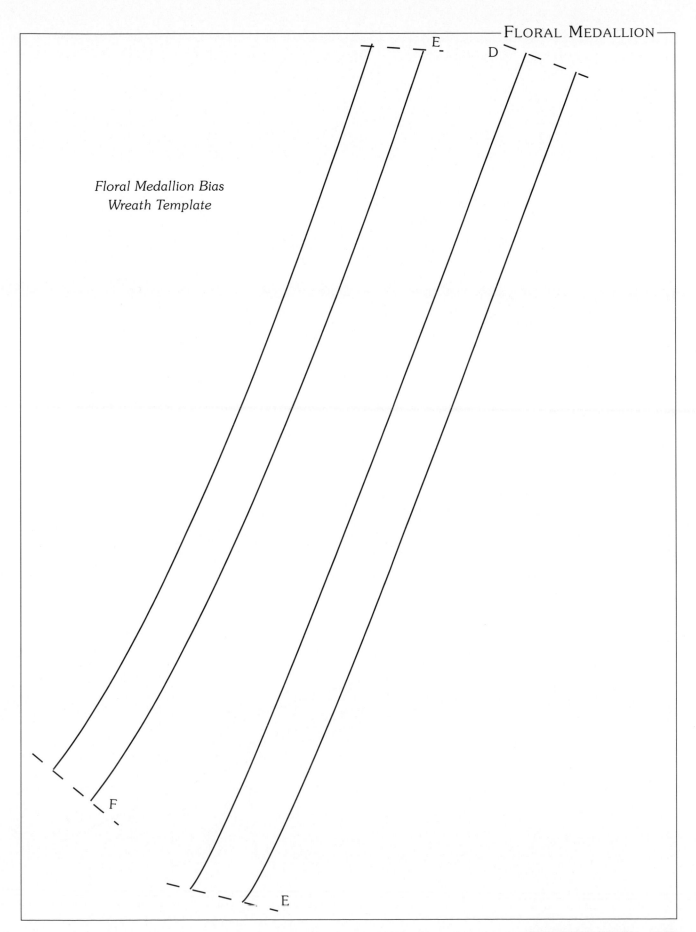

*Floral Medallion Bias
Wreath Template*

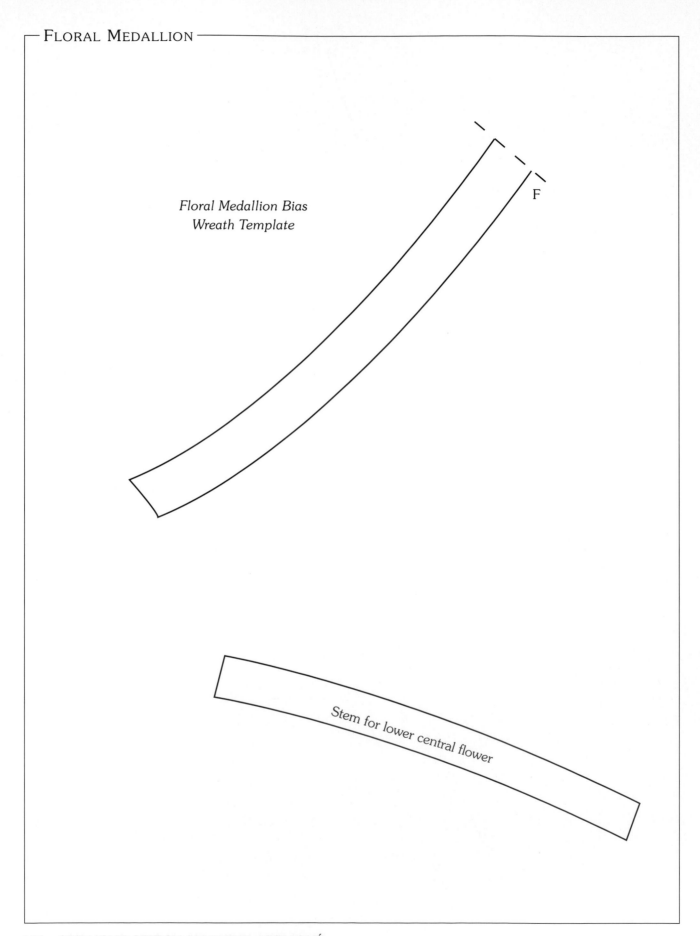

*Floral Medallion Bias
Wreath Template*

F

Stem for lower central flower

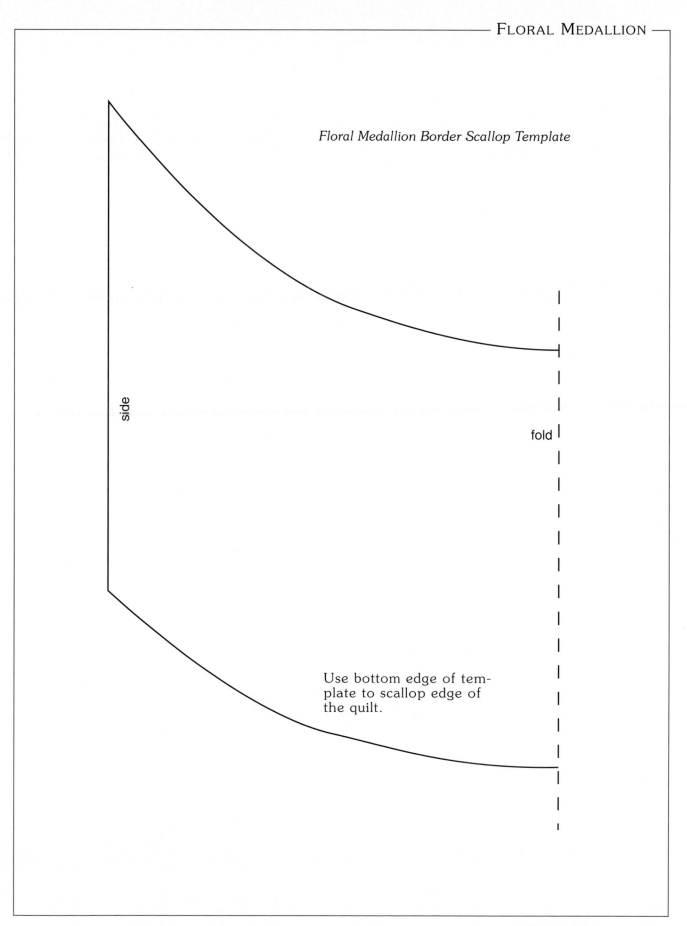

Floral Medallion Border Scallop Template

side

fold

Use bottom edge of template to scallop edge of the quilt.

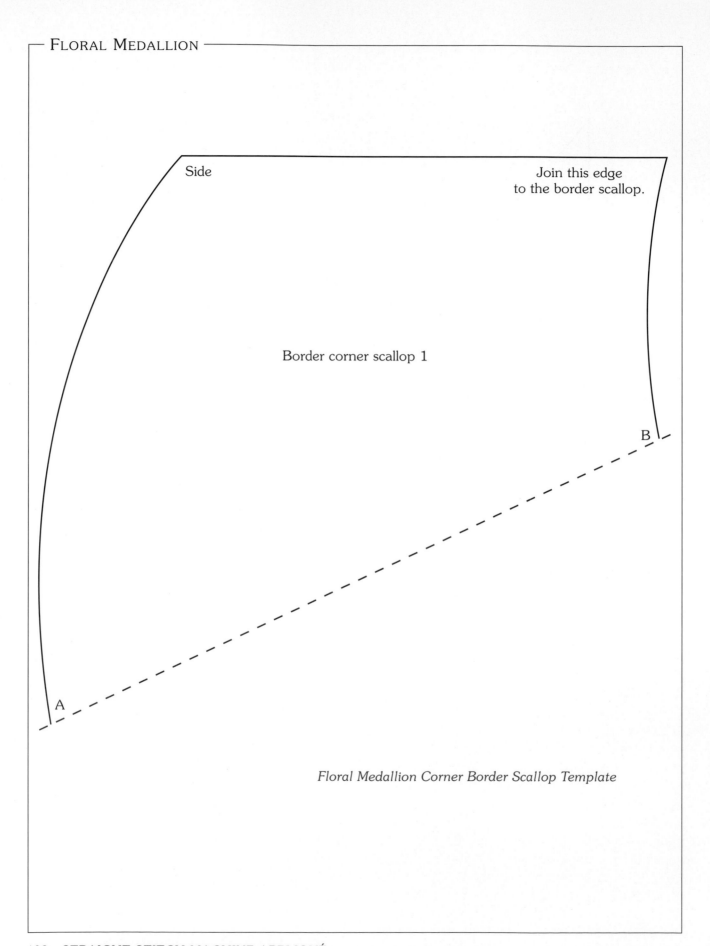

Side

Join this edge
to the border scallop.

Border corner scallop 1

B

A

Floral Medallion Corner Border Scallop Template

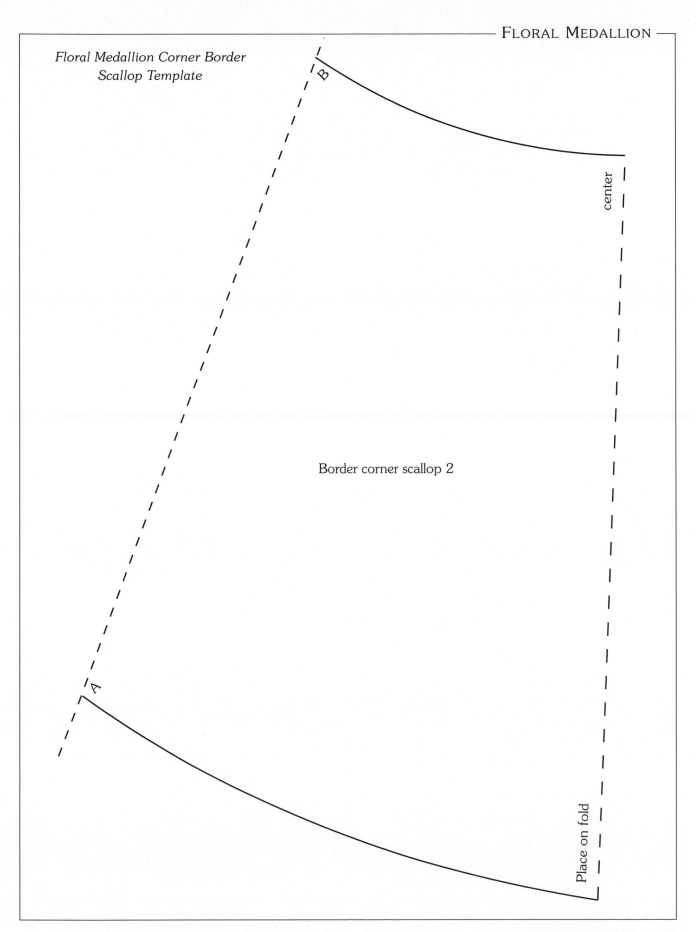

*Floral Medallion Corner Border
Scallop Template*

B

center

Border corner scallop 2

A

Place on fold

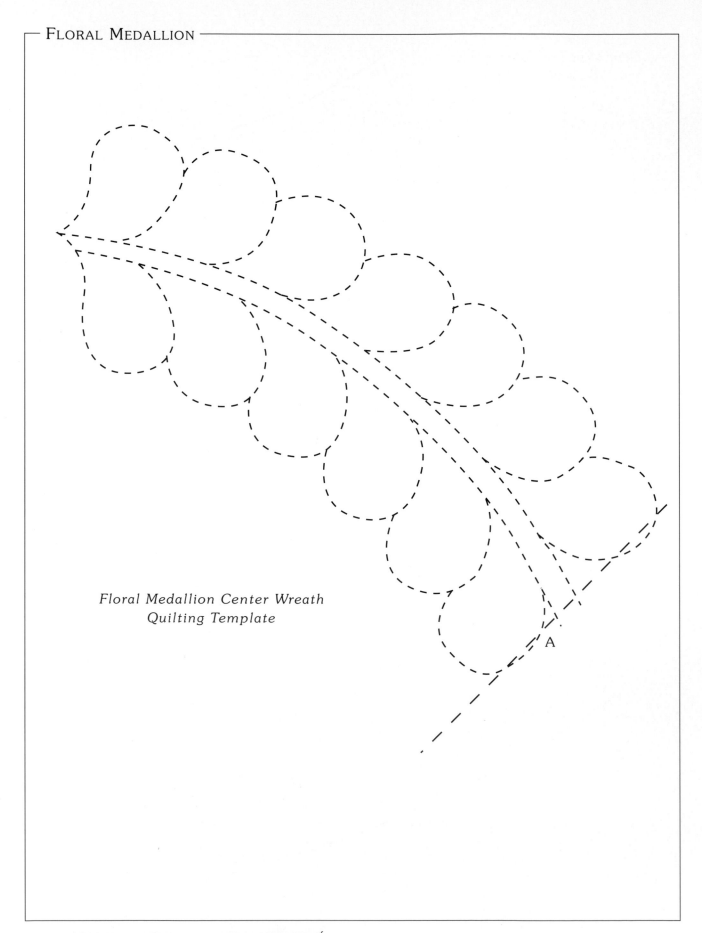

*Floral Medallion Center Wreath
Quilting Template*

A

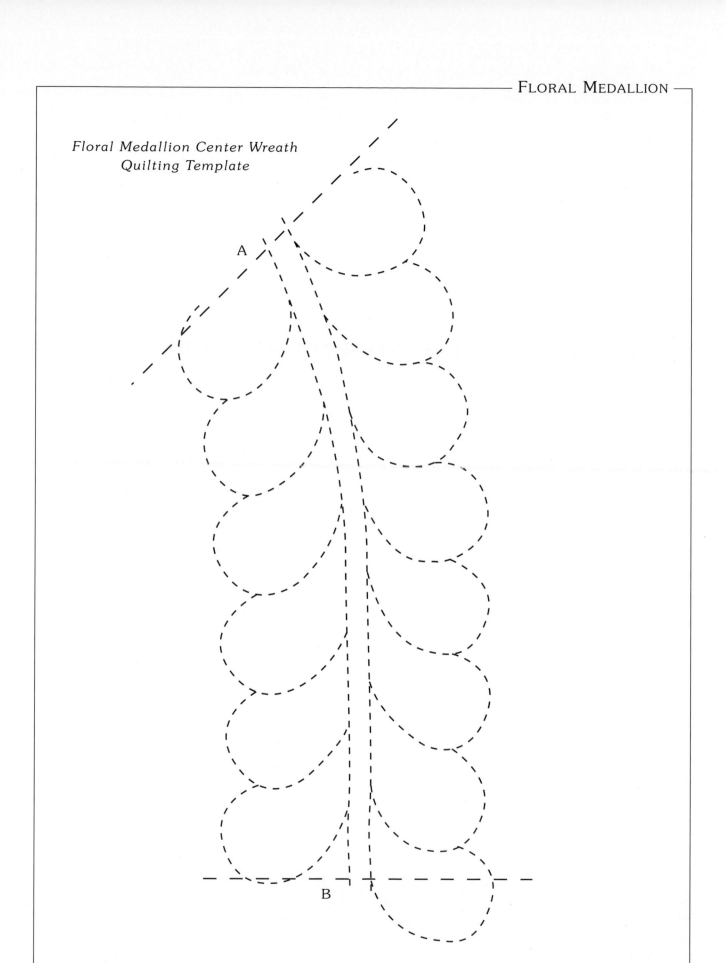

Floral Medallion Center Wreath
Quilting Template

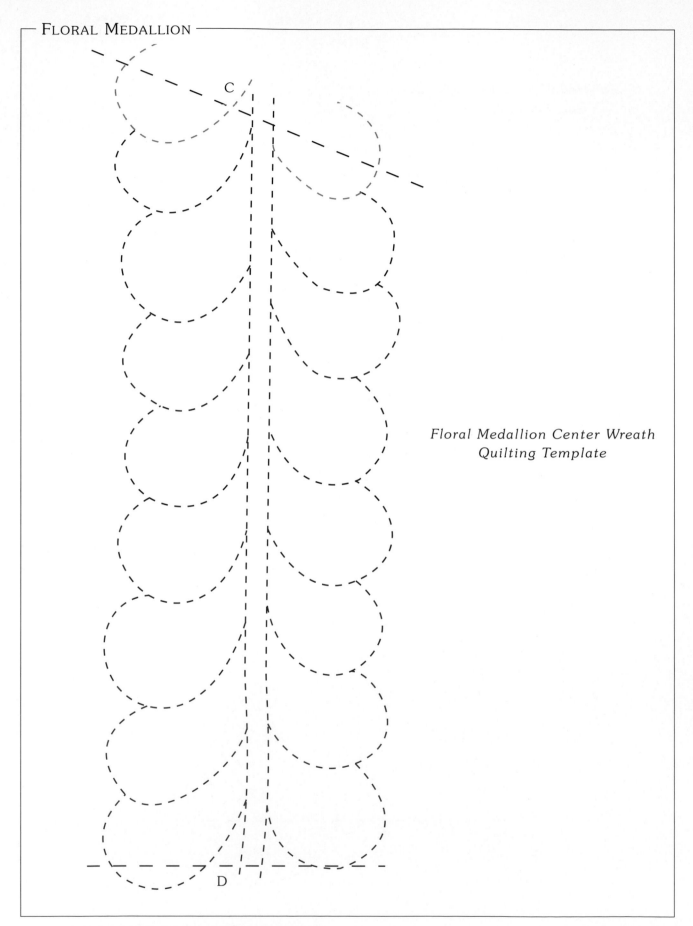

C

D

*Floral Medallion Center Wreath
Quilting Template*

*Floral Medallion Center Wreath
Quilting Template*

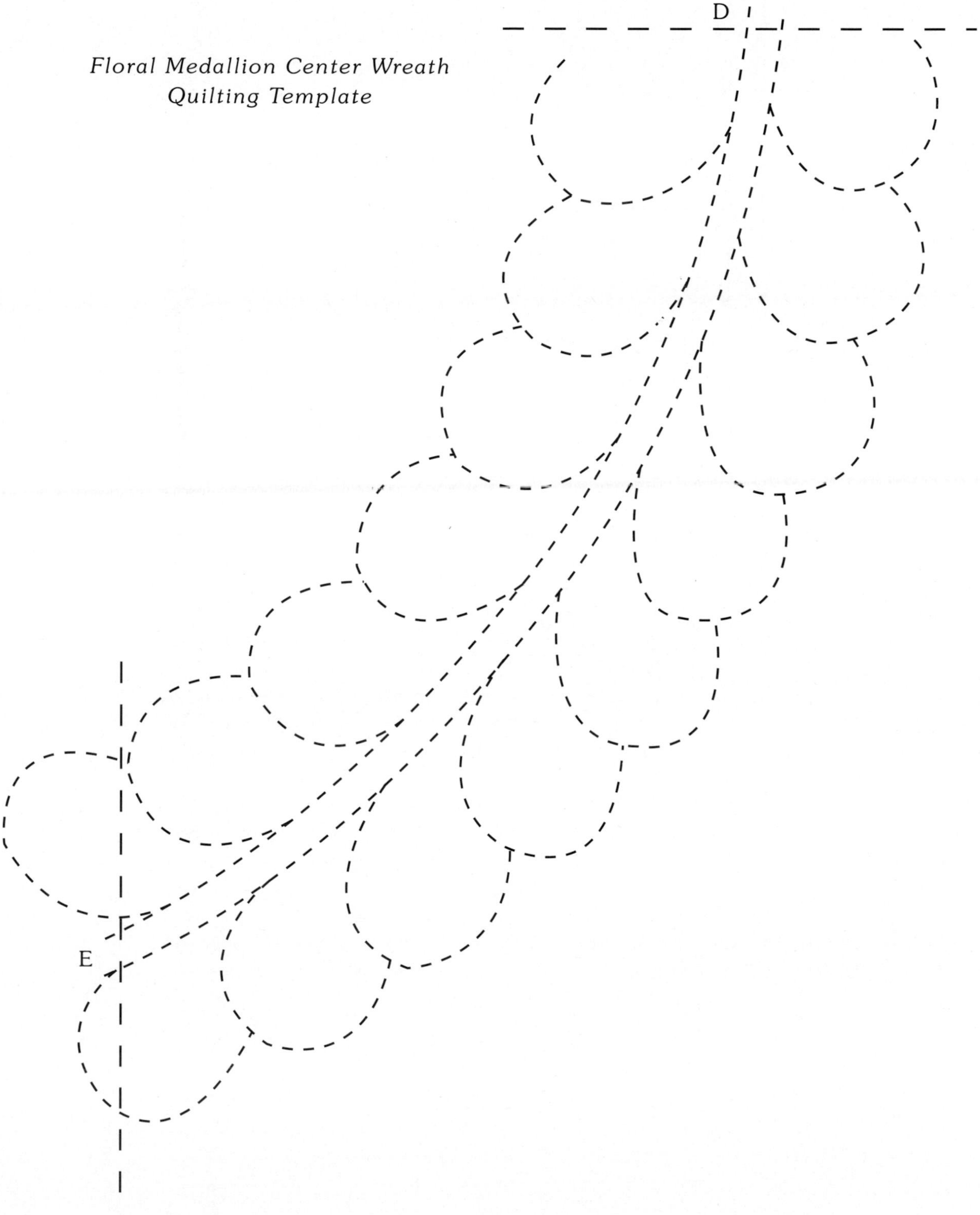

D

E

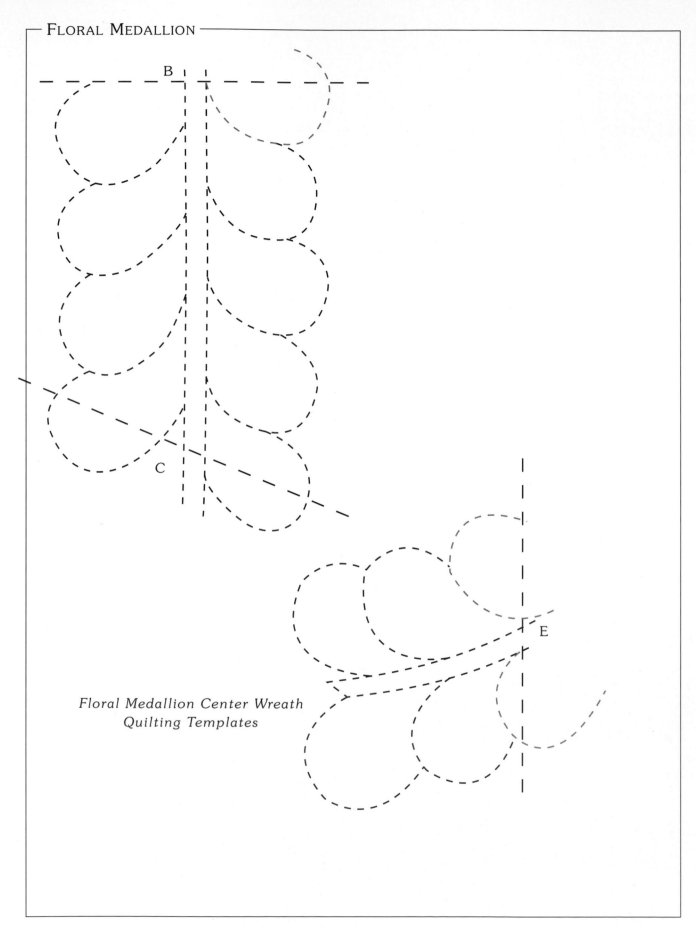

*Floral Medallion Center Wreath
Quilting Templates*

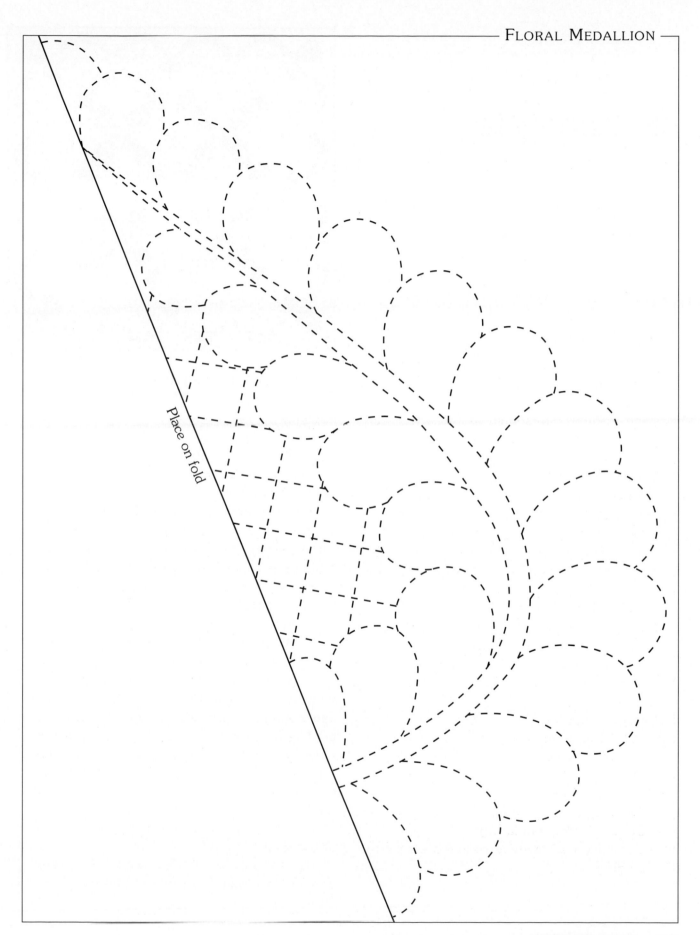

Place on fold

Pineapple

56½" x 56½"

LEVEL: INTERMEDIATE

Color photo on page 46.

The pineapple, signifying warmth, welcome, and hospitality becomes the perfect Christmas quilt. This easy-to-appliqué Pineapple quilt makes a dramatic statement done in bold colors such as red and green. Other colors are equally handsome.

YARDAGE

6½ yds. pale yellow print for background and backing
1 yd. red print
1 yd. green solid
81" x 96" quilt batt

CUTTING INSTRUCTIONS

Background fabric:
    Cut two 10½" x 36½" border strips
    Cut two 10½" x 57½" border strips
    Cut four 18½" squares

Red print fabric:
    Cut 20 A, pineapple
    Cut 16 E, swags

Green solid fabric:
    Cut 4 D, center squares
    Cut 24 C, pineapple tops
    Cut seven 2" wide crosswise strips for binding

METHOD OF CONSTRUCTION

1. Prepare each 18½" square for appliqué by folding in half and quarter, finger press. Also fold diagonally and finger press. Prepare the shapes for appliqué. Use the fold lines to help center and place the appliqué pieces.

2. Machine appliqué each block in the following order beginning with D, the center square, corners on fold lines, C, pineapple tops (center tip should be 2½" from the corner of the block), and last A, the pineapple.

3. Sew the four large blocks together.

4. Make the borders following these directions. Appliqué these shapes onto the borders first, before adding borders to the quilt top. On each 36½" border strip, center and appliqué a pineapple top. The tip will be 1" from the cut edge of the border. On either side of the pineapple top appliqué one swag. The tip will be 4½" from the top cut edge of the border, the bottom 1" from the bottom cut edge of the border.

5. Sew these borders to opposite sides of the quilt top.

6. To each of the 57½" borders appliqué a pineapple top and two swags on either side.

7. Sew these last two borders to the top and bottom of the quilt top. Finger press a diagonal miter line from the corner of the quilt top out through the border to the quilt tops corner. Center a pineapple top along this fold line, its tip 1¼" from border seam line. Appliqué in place. Center pineapple, its bottom 4" from the corner. Appliqué in place.

8. Mark for quilting. A feathered wreath is between each block. Radiating out from the quilt's center, mark parallel lines 1¼" apart. Using the pineapple top as a pattern, mark design where ends of the appliquéd swags meet on the border. Use swag templates to mark curved lines 1" apart between the appliquéd swags and around corner pineapple. See Figure 28. Quilt pineapple and center as shown in Figure 29.

9. After quilting is completed, bind the edges with green.

Figure 28.

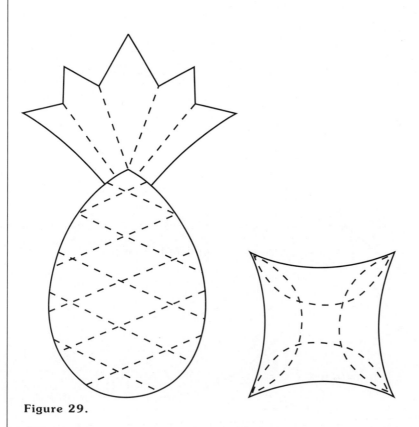

Figure 29.

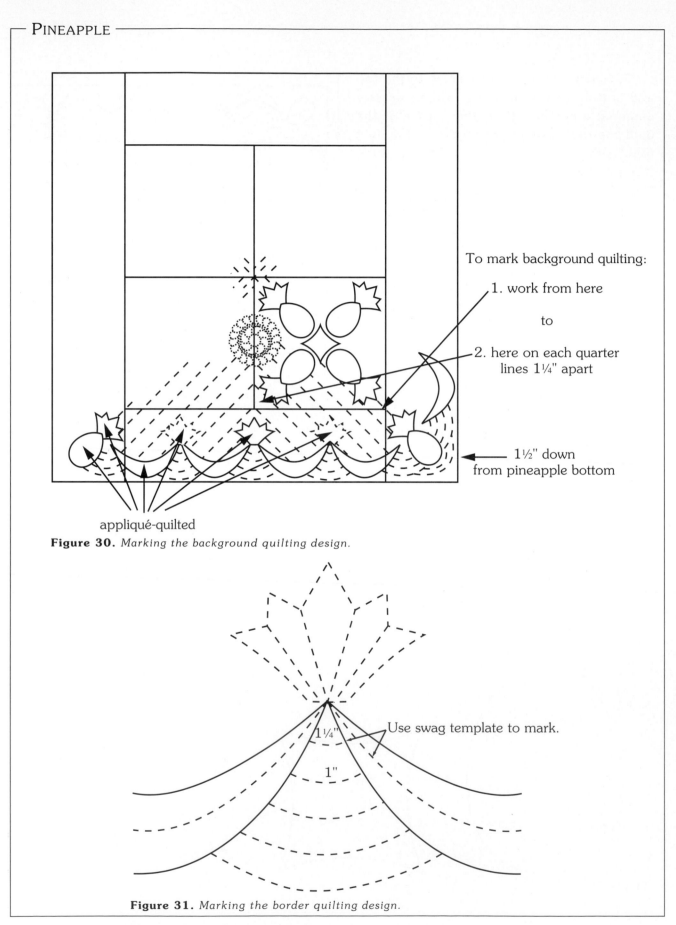

To mark background quilting:

1. work from here

to

2. here on each quarter
lines 1¼" apart

1½" down
from pineapple bottom

appliqué-quilted

Figure 30. *Marking the background quilting design.*

Use swag template to mark.

1¼"

1"

Figure 31. *Marking the border quilting design.*

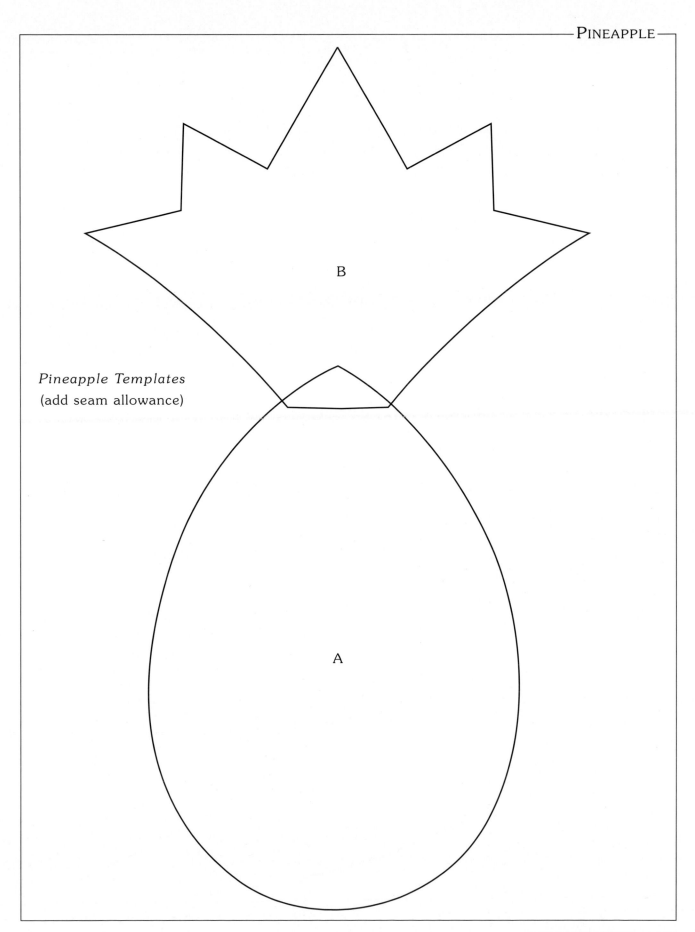

Pineapple Templates
(add seam allowance)

B

A

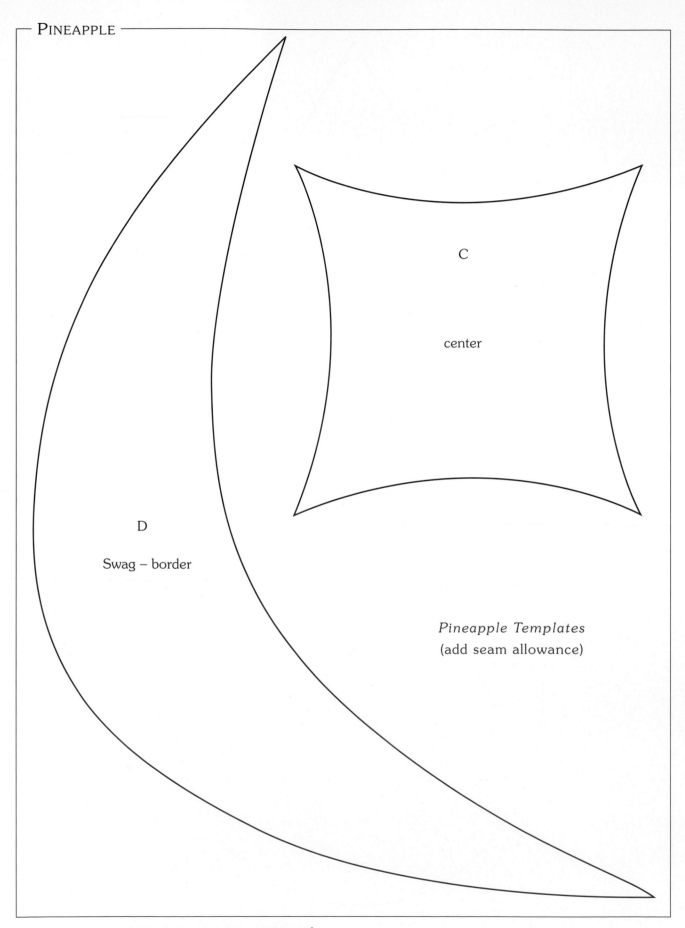

C

center

D

Swag – border

Pineapple Templates
(add seam allowance)

Pineapple Quilting Template

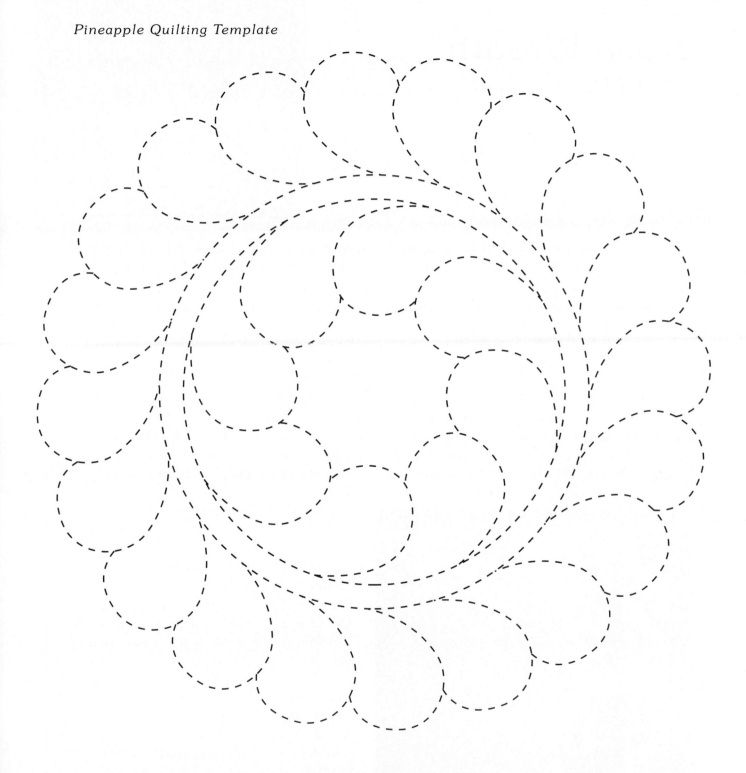

Rose Wreath

48" x 48"

LEVEL: EASY

Color photo on page 47.

In the early twentieth-century selling quilt patterns became a business. Previously women acquired new quilt patterns mainly by trading with each other, seeing a quilt they liked at a county fair and copying the idea, or creating their own designs. Newspapers printed pictures of quilt block patterns, kits became available, and patterns were sold. This pattern sold by the Wonderart Company of Chicago, Illinois, for the Rose Wreath, c. 1930, contained precut fabric to be appliquéd to a stamped background block. Placement lines for the appliqué as well as dots indicating quilting lines were stamped on the block. Brief instructions were given on the back of the package, and the company advised 20 packages were needed to complete the quilt. The quilt block package sold for 10 cents!

YARDAGE

3 yds. medium pink solid for background blocks and borders

1 yd. black print for flowers, buds and binding

½ yd. taupe solid for stems, vines and leaves

¼ yd. each of a medium and light print for leaves

CUTTING INSTRUCTIONS

Medium pink solid:

  Cut four 16½" background blocks
  Cut four 2" x 16½" strips for inner border
  Cut four 6½" x 48½" outer border strips
  Cut 16 B's, flower centers

Black print:

  Cut 20 A's, flowers
  Cut 8 D's, buds *
  Cut five 2" wide crosswise strips for binding
  *Cut one 2" x 21" strip each of black print and taupe fabrics. Sew together on the long edges. Press seam toward taupe.

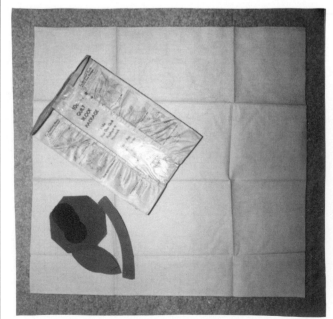

Plate 63.

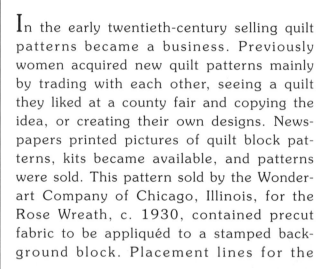

From this strip cut the whole bud, match dotted line on template to seam line on the fabric strip.

Taupe solid:
  Cut 16 C's, leaves
  Cut 10¼ yds. 1⅛" wide bias strips for wreath and vining border

Medium print:
  Cut 48 C's, leaves
  Cut eight 2" x 10½" strips for inner border

Light print:
  Cut 16 C's, leaves

METHOD OF CONSTRUCTION

1. Mark background blocks for placement of appliqué pieces.

2. Prepare bias and appliqué pieces. Appliqué bias strips for wreath, sewing the inner curve first. Prepare B, center circle and appliqué to the flower A. Appliqué flower unit to the block. Appliqué the leaves, C in place. Appliqué four blocks. Sew the four blocks together.

3. Prepare the inner border by sewing a strip of medium print fabric 2" x 10½" to each end of a pink strip, 2" x 16½". Make four strips.

4. Sew each of the inner border strips (made in Step 3) to a pink outer border.

5. Make a paper pattern of the appliqué border design. Place the fabric borders over the pattern and mark the fabric for placement of the various appliqué pieces. Appliqué the short stems first, then buds, and leaves. Sew borders to the quilt top. Miter corners. Appliqué the vine around the entire border.

6. Layer the quilt.

7. Quilt around each appliqué piece. Quilt flower motif in center of quilt. Quilt one inch cross hatching in the center of the wreaths and on the narrow inner border. Quilt the small cable between the blocks. Use the leaf appliqué template for marking those shapes on the border. Quilt the remaining flower and leaf designs as shown in drawing.

8. Bind the edges with black print binding.

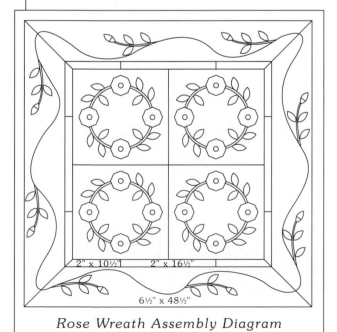

Rose Wreath Assembly Diagram

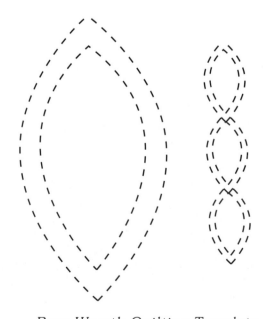

Rose Wreath Quilting Template

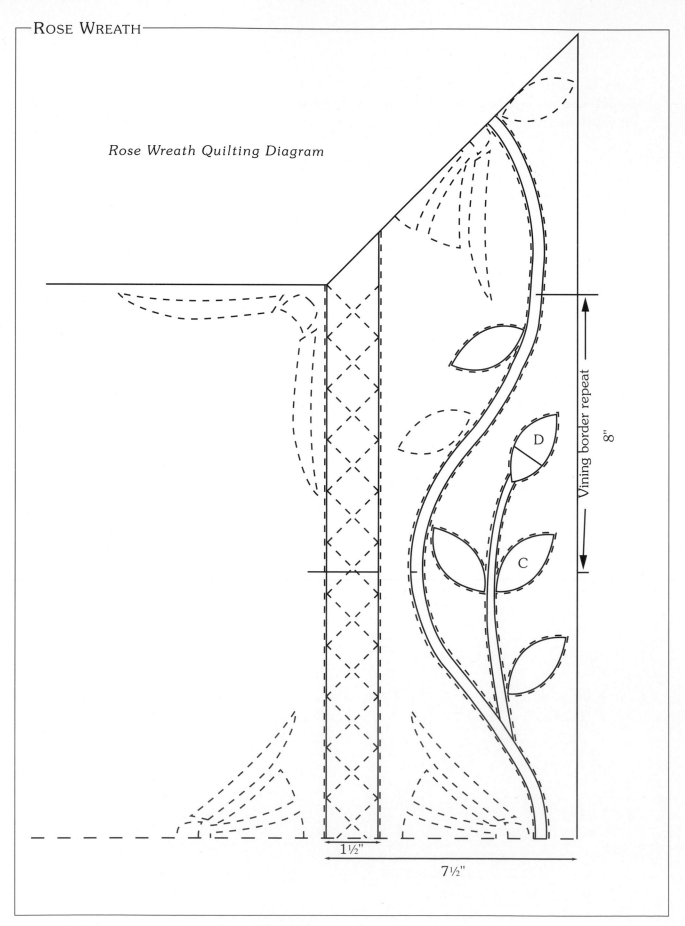

Rose Wreath Quilting Diagram

D

C

Vining border repeat

8"

1½"

7½"

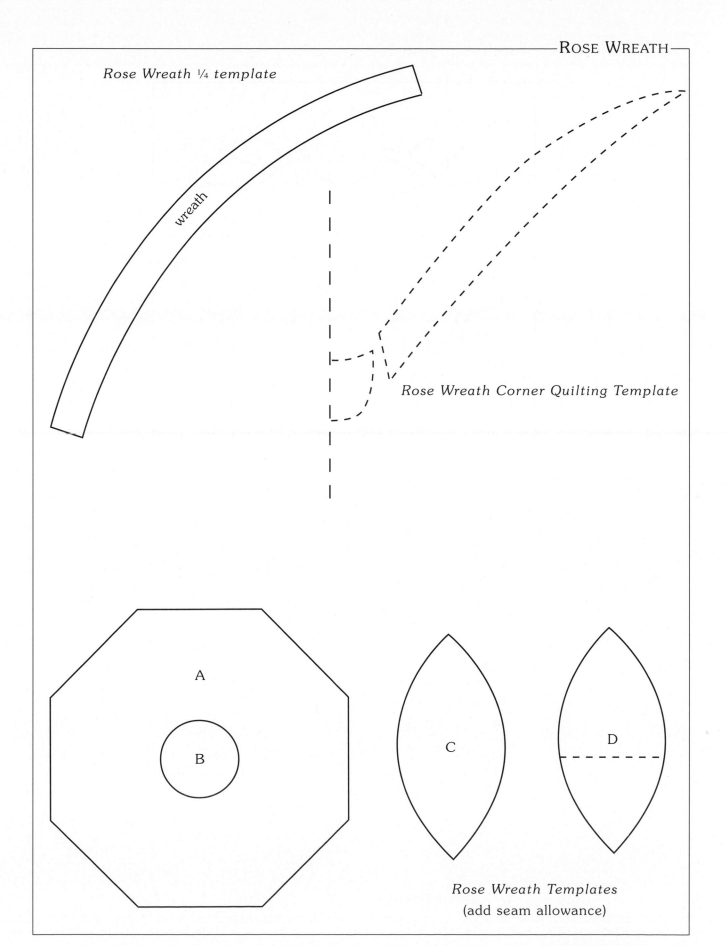

Rose Wreath ¼ template

wreath

Rose Wreath Corner Quilting Template

A

B

C

D

Rose Wreath Templates
(add seam allowance)

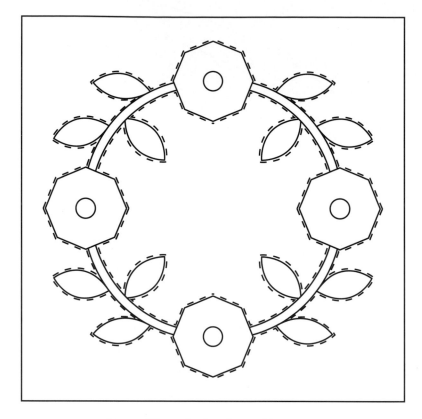

Rose Wreath Quilting Diagram

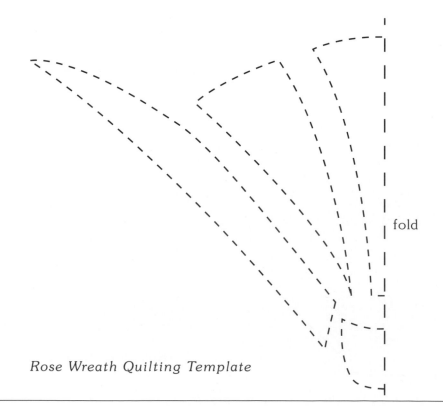

fold

Rose Wreath Quilting Template

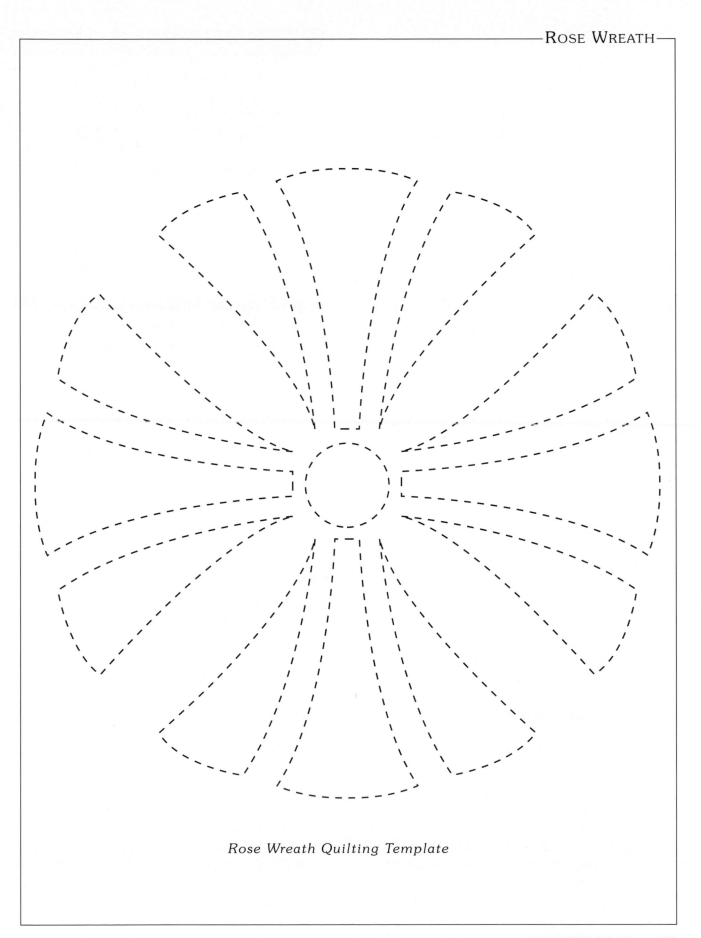

Rose Wreath Quilting Template

Double Peony and Rose

88" x 107"

LEVEL: INTERMEDIATE

Color photo on page 50.

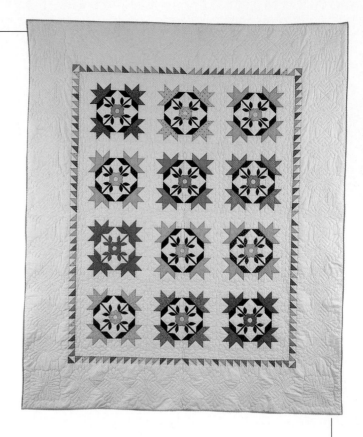

The Double Peony and Rose is a pattern which combines appliqué and piecing. Dramatic in red and green as shown, it would be equally stunning in deep pink and green.

YARDAGE

9 yds. muslin for background
3½ yds. red print for blocks, border, and binding
1 yd. green print for stems and leaves
⅛ yd. yellow for flower centers
6½ yds. muslin for backing
90" x 108" queen size batt

CUTTING INSTRUCTIONS

Cutting instructions for use without templates follow, but if you prefer to use templates, patterns are also given.

Muslin:
  For borders and sashing
    Cut two 11½" x 107½" outer borders strips
    Cut two 11½" x 88½" outer borders strips
    Cut eight 3½" x 16½" sashing strips
    Cut three 3½" x 54½" sashing strips
    Cut two 3½" x 60½" inner border strips
    Cut two 3½" x 79½" inner border strips

Cut six 2⅞" wide strips. Cut into seventy 2⅞" squares. Cut each square into two triangles – 140 D's for Sawtooth border.

For Blocks:
  Cut 48 A's (Cut three 2½" wide strips. Cut into forty-eight 2½" squares.)
  Cut 144 B's (Cut five 5¼" wide strips. Cut into thirty-six 5¼" squares. Cut each square into four triangles = 144 triangles.)
  Cut 48 C's (Cut six 2½" wide strips. Cut into forty-eight 4½" lengths.)
  Cut 12 G's (Cut three 8½" wide strips. Cut into twelve 8½" squares.)

Red print:
  Cut 428 D's & Sawtooth border (Cut sixteen 2⅞" wide strips.) Cut into 214 – 2⅞" squares, then cut into 428 triangles, 288 are D's used in the blocks and 140 are used for the Sawtooth border.
  Cut 48 E's (Cut three 2½" wide strips. Cut into forty-eight 2½" squares.)
  Cut 12 K's

Green print:
  Cut 192 F's (Cut seven 2⅞" wide strips. Cut into ninety-six 2⅞" squares, then cut into 192 triangles.)
  Cut 48 H's (Cut five 1⅛" strips for stems. Prepare for appliqué and cut into 4½" lengths.)
  Cut 96 I's

Yellow:
  Cut 12 J's

METHOD OF CONSTRUCTION

1. Prepare pieces H, I, J, K for appliqué. For each block you will need 4 H's, 8 I's 1 J, and 1 K. Appliqué to background block G in the following order: H to G, J to K, K to G, and I to G. See Figure 32. Appliqué 12 blocks.

2. Refer to Figure 33 to see how to piece the remaining sections of the block.

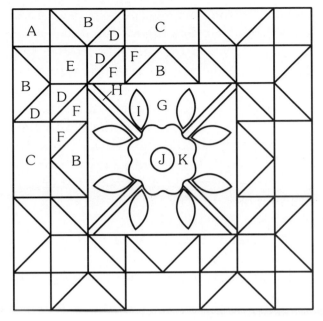

Figure 33. *Assembly guide for Double Peony and Rose.*

Figure 32. *Appliqué stems, flowers, and leaves to 8½" block.*

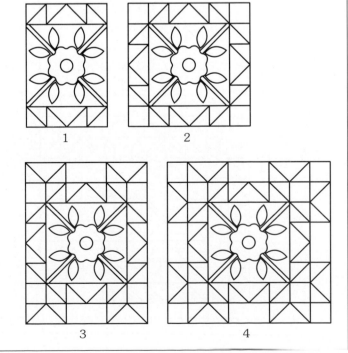

3. To piece the Sawtooth border place a red and a muslin triangle right sides together, sew on the long edge. Chain sew 140 of these triangles. See Figure 34. Press seam to the red side. Notice that the red triangles reverse directions at the center of each border and that the corners have the red triangle facing the outside. Sew triangles into long strips for the Sawtooth border. Each side border has 38 triangles, and the end borders plus corners have 32 triangles.

Figure 34.

4. Arrange blocks and sashing as shown in picture. Join three Double Peony and Rose blocks with 3½" x 16½" sashing strips between. Prepare four rows. Press seam allowance toward sashing.

5. Join rows of pieced blocks with a strip of 3½" x 54½" sashing in between each row. Press seams toward sashing. Make sure blocks and sashing strips in row one line up with those in row two, and each successive row.

6. Add inner borders, mitering corners.

7. Add Sawtooth border.

8. Add outer borders, mitering borders.

9. Mark for quilting as shown and layer the quilt. Quilt feathers in sashing. Quilt ¼" from seam line on white triangles in sawtooth border. Using border motif, combine two designs to be quilted in the corners of border. Mark a border design. Evenly space nine motifs on long borders, seven on short borders. Join with angled lines spaced ¾" apart as shown.

10. Bind with remaining red fabric.

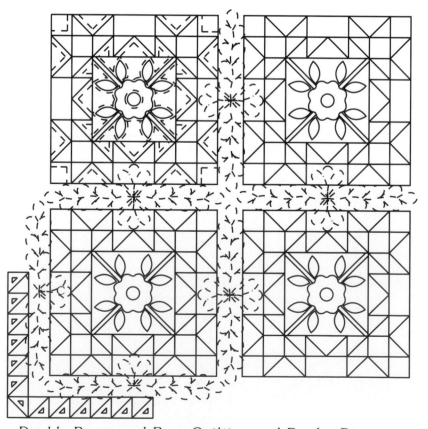

Double Peony and Rose Quilting and Border Diagram

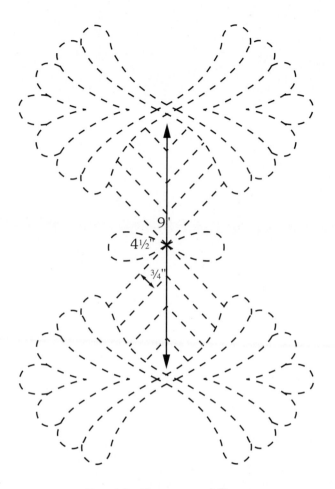

9'

4½"

¾"

Double Peony and Rose
Quilting Diagrams

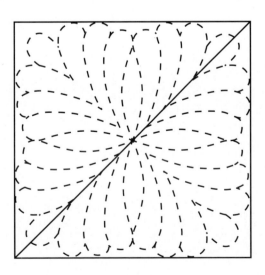

Double Peony and Rose
Quilting Template

fold

*Double Peony and Rose
Quilting Diagram*

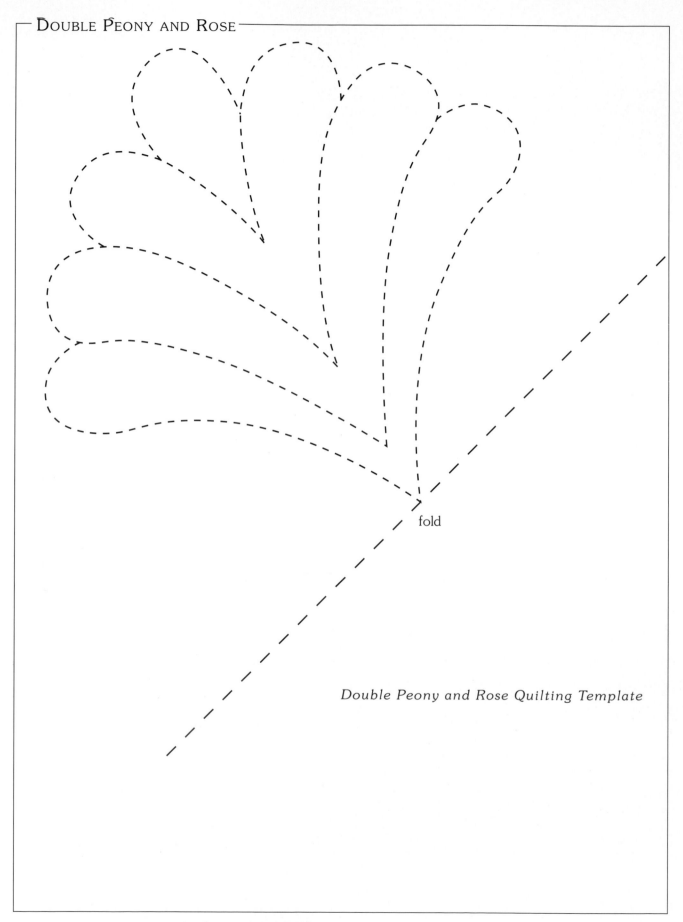

fold

Double Peony and Rose Quilting Template

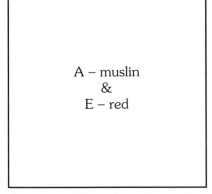

A – muslin
&
E – red

Double Peony and Rose Templates
(add seam allowance)

D – red
&
F – green

H – 8½" square of muslin

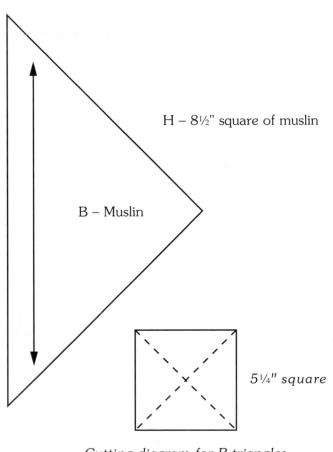

B – Muslin

C – Muslin

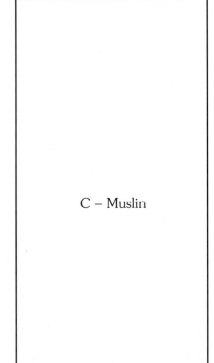

5¼" square

Cutting diagram for B triangles

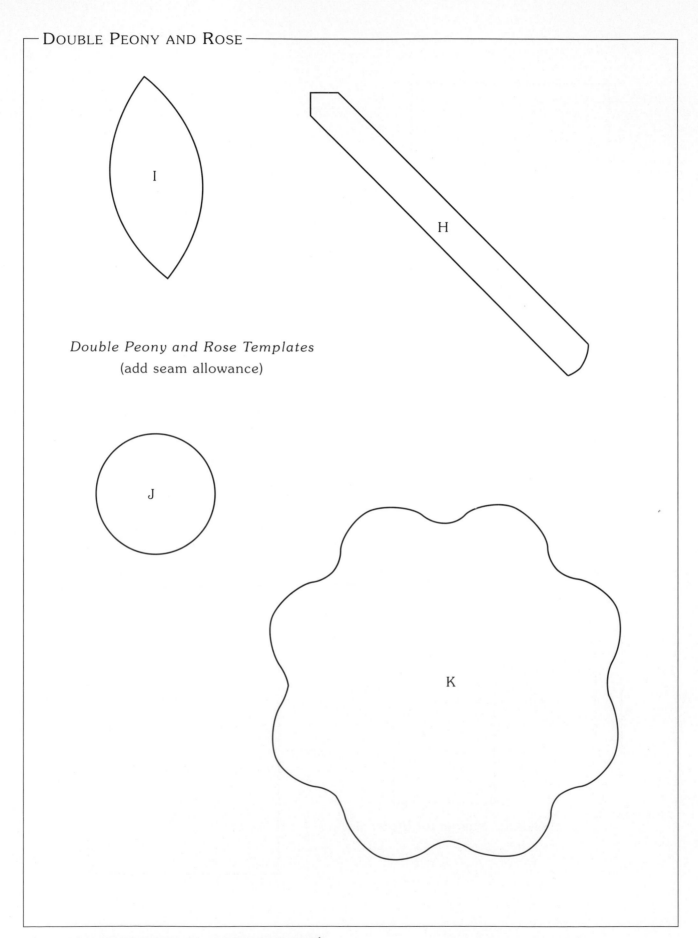

Double Peony and Rose Templates
(add seam allowance)

APPENDIX
FINISHING THE QUILT

Plate 64. *SUNBONNET SUE, 65" x 90". Machine appliqué.*

QUILT BLOCK SETTINGS

Many of the quilt blocks in this book are set in one of two ways, block to block or on point. Those quilt blocks set in other special ways are discussed with the individual patterns.

Quilt blocks can be sewn together block to block or they may have sashing, or strips of material, separating the blocks, however the sequence of quilt block assembly will be the same.

BLOCK TO BLOCK

Lay out the quilt blocks on a large surface such as a bed, table, or floor. Arrange the blocks for a pleasing placement of colors if necessary. Also include the sashing if part of the quilt. Sew together in horizontal rows. If seam allowances are pressed in opposite directions in each row, seam lines will easily and accurately line up when the rows are sewn together. See Figure 34.

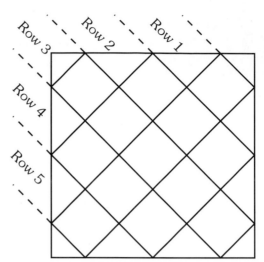

Figure 35. *Quilt layout with blocks set on point.*

angles on a large surface. Arrange the blocks placing colors where you like them. Quilt blocks, set on point are sewn together in diagonal rows. Sew the corner triangles on last. Beginning with the block in the upper right hand corner (Row 1), sew a side setting triangle to opposite sides of the block. Return the strip to its place in the quilt block arrangement. Refering to the drawing, continue to sew the blocks and side setting triangles together in diagonal rows. See Figure 35. Press seam allowances in each row in opposite directions. See Figure 36. Sew rows together into groups of two, then four, continuing

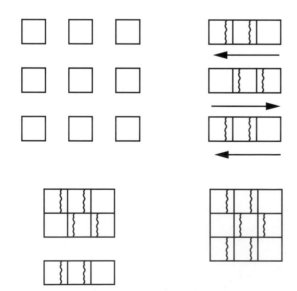

Figure 34. *Pressing seam allowance in opposite directions in block to block setting.*

ON POINT

To assemble the quilt top first lay out all the blocks and side and corner setting tri-

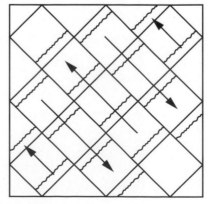

Figure 36. *Seam allowances pressed in opposite directions of blocks set on point.*

on until the quilt top is sewn together. Add borders as described below if they are a part of the quilt you are making.

BORDERS

Once you have the quilt blocks sewn together, adding the borders is the next step, if your quilt is to have a border. Not all quilts need to have borders. A border can make a quilt larger, without your having to make extra blocks. It can also act as a frame for the blocks, giving a finished look to the quilt. By repeating in the border a fabric that was used in the blocks, a unifying effect is created. Wide plain borders provide a large area for fancy quilting, which can give a very elegant look to your quilt.

Experiment with your quilt top by folding lengthwise a couple yards of potential border fabric and placing it next to the quilt top's edge. This will show you what a border of a certain color and design will look like. If you are thinking about multiple borders, fold several lengths of fabric to the approximate widths you want to consider, and lay them next to the top's edge. Sometimes you may want to leave this border arrangement set up for several hours or overnight to see if it is the one you really like. Once you have decided on a border you can cut the fabric and sew it to the quilt top.

Borders on each side of the quilt top should be cut the same length before being sewn to the quilt. This will let the quilt hang evenly and corners will be square. To know how long to cut the borders, first measure the quilt top in three places along its width and length. Measure across each side and across the middle of the quilt top, on both the length and width. Compare the three measurements of the length. They may differ slightly. If they vary no more than an inch, use the center measurement

as the length to cut the border fabric. Repeat for the width measurements. Usually the center measurement of the quilt will give a pretty true size of the quilt.

If the dimensions are slightly different, this means one edge of the quilt top might need to be stretched slightly to fit the border and the other eased slightly to fit. If the end or side quilt measurements differ a lot more than one inch, you should make corrections within the quilt top before adding the borders.

Before cutting the borders, decide on the corner treatment you plan to use. Whether you are using set-in blocks, mitered, or butted or straight seam corners will effect the length your borders should be cut. See Figure 37.

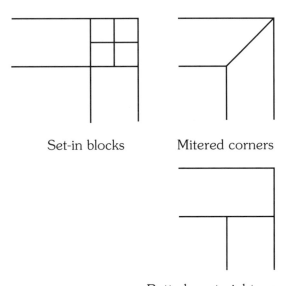

Set-in blocks   Mitered corners

Butted or straight seam

Figure 37.

SET-IN CORNER BLOCKS

The RABBIT'S PAW quilt shows set-in blocks for a corner treatment. A portion of the quilt block was used for these corners. This type of corner gives unity to a quilt. The borders in this case will be cut the length and width of the quilt, as described above, plus ½" seam allowance. Let us look at a quilt top which is 36" x 36" and to have an 8" wide border. Each border would be cut 36½" x 8½". The corner blocks which are a square the same width as the borders, would be cut 8½" square. They are sewn to the end of the borders. Sew the side borders to the quilt top, then the end borders, matching corner seam lines.

Set-in corner blocks could also be a solid piece of fabric (not a pieced block) in a color or pattern that complements the quilt top. Borders using a set-in corner block can be different widths. This type of border and corner arrangement could be useful if you are short of fabric for the border lengths. Amish quilts frequently have set-in corner blocks. See Figure 38.

BUTTED OR STRAIGHT SEAM

Borders with butted or straight seam corners are easy to add to a quilt top and can be used when borders are different widths. They also require less fabric than borders with mitered corner seams. The OAK LEAF AND REEL (page 15) is an example of outer borders being different widths. The 1930's TULIP has inner muslin borders of different widths. This was done to make the quilt top the correct size so the pieced border would fit. It also floats the quilt top, or separates it from the border design. Corner treatments generally should be the same for all the borders that may be in a quilt top, this being another way of giving unity to the quilt top.

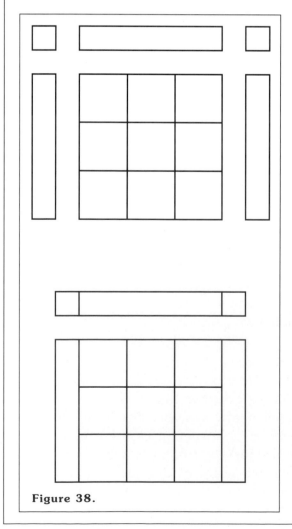

Figure 38.

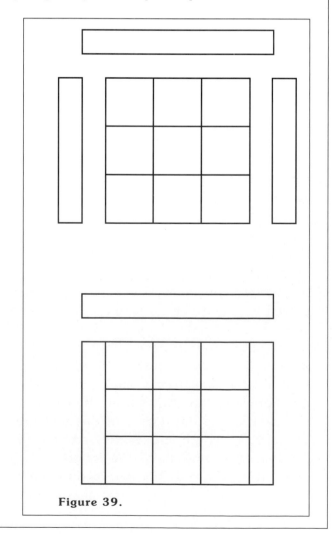

Figure 39.

Side borders are cut the finished length of the quilt, plus ½", this allows for a quarter inch seam allowance at each end of the border. For example let's measure and cut borders on a quilt top which is 36" x 36" and to have 8" borders. Side borders would be cut 36½" x 8½". End borders are cut the finished width of the quilt, plus the finished width of each side border, plus ½". Adding the dimensions ¼" + 8" + 36" + 8" + ¼" = 52½", which is the length to cut the end borders. Sew on the side borders first, then the end borders. See Figure 39.

Butted or straight seam borders can also be sewn as shown in Figure 40. Borders have been sewn to the top and bottom first, and then the side borders were added. If this option is used, remember the borders will need to be cut different lengths than those shown in Cutting Instructions.

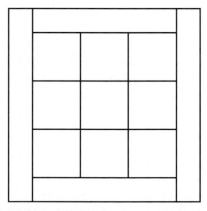

Figure 40. *Example of top and bottom borders sewn on before side borders.*

Mitered Corners

Mitered corners have their corner seams joined on a 45° angle. Mitered corners need to have borders which are of equal widths. Borders with mitered corners require the most fabric of the three examples we are considering. They each need to be the length of the quilt, plus twice the

width of the border, plus ½" seam allowance.

Let us look at an example of a quilt top which is 36" x 36" and will have an eight inch border. The length is 36" plus an 8" border at each end or 16", plus ½" for seam allowances for a total of 52½". It is a good idea to add a little extra length, about 2", so you will cut the four borders each 54½" long. See Figure 41.

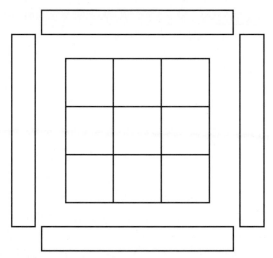

Figure 41.

To sew mitered borders to the quilt top, begin by folding or measuring to find a center for each border and edge of the quilt top. Either crease or mark the centers with a pin. On the border also measure and mark with pins the finished length of the quilt top, matching the center of the border with the center of the measurement. The finished length of the quilt top does not include the seam allowances. With right sides together, pin the center of a border to the center edge of the quilt top. Also pin the ends of the border to the quilt top as measured. Pin as needed in between, easing in any extra fullness or stretching if necessary. If any fullness needs to be eased, when sewing have that side next to the feed dogs on the sewing machine. It will help to evenly ease in the extra fabric. You will sew these borders on from seam line to seam line. Begin sewing ¼" from the corner and sew to ¼" of the next corner. Backstitch and clip threads. Repeat sewing on all four borders. See Figure 42.

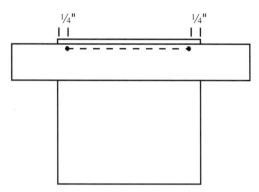

Figure 42.

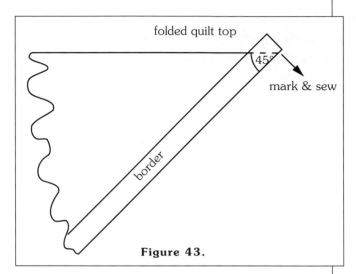

Figure 43.

Fold the quilt top, right sides together, so two adjacent borders form a 45° angle. Carefully align borders, realigning allowance where you stopped sewing at the corners. Mark a 45° angle on the wrong side of one border. Mark from where you stopped sewing the borders out to the cut edge of the border. See Figure 43. Pin and carefully sew on your marked line. Repeat for all four corners. Spread the quilt top flat on a large surface. Check to see if the corners are square and borders lie flat. If so, press seams to one side and trim seam allowance to ¼". If the mitered seam does not lie flat or the border has ripples, examine the mitered corner seam to see if your angle is a true 45°. If the border ripples, it is probably slightly too long. You may need to re-mark the corner mitered seam and sew again.

STRAIGHT STITCH MACHINE
APPLIQUÉ BORDERS

It is easiest to appliqué borders before they are sewn to the quilt top because there is less material to be maneuvered around at the sewing machine. Therefore, measure the borders to determine their correct length. Refer to the sections on borders to help with these measurements.

Making a paper pattern of the border will let you trace appliqué placement marks to the border fabric, much as you did with the appliqué blocks. It may be necessary to make a separate pattern for the end and side borders. Your paper pattern for the border should be the finished measurements of the border. Use a pencil to work out the design. You can trace around the plastic templates used in the blocks if they are the correct size or cut new templates in the size and shape you want to use in the border. Then go over the pencil lines on the paper pattern with a black pen so the design will easily show through the fabric. The darker the black lines the more easily they will show through the fabric. See Plate 65. A light table is especially helpful if the fabric is a print or a medium or dark color.

Pin the border fabric to the paper pattern. Use the Berol® silver pencil to mark the placement of the appliqué pieces. Remember to use only a few reference marks – V marks for each end of the leaves,

Plate 65. *Darken quilting lines on pattern. Photo: Letty Martin.*

Plate 67. *After appliquéing, sew borders to quilt top. Photo: Letty Martin.*

or dashes for one side of a stem or vine.

Using the sewing machine, straight stitch machine appliqué as many of the border pieces in place as you can before sewing the border to the quilt top. See Plate 66.

Vines and pieces which cross seams will need to be appliquéd on after the borders are sewn to the quilt top.

Once you have appliquéd as many pieces to the borders as possible, sew the borders to the quilt top. See Plate 67.

Pin in place the additional appliqué shapes. Fold the quilt top into a small pack-

age leaving a border area free. Straight stitch machine appliqué on desired shapes. See Plate 68.

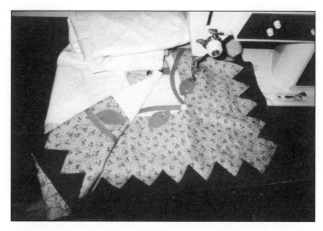

Plate 68. *Completing appliqué over seam lines. Photo: Letty Martin.*

If a vine is being appliquéd, refold the quilt top as necessary to continue sewing around the quilt. Join the ends of a continuous vine as described in the section on sewing bias bindings to scalloped edges.

DOGTOOTH BORDERS

The Dogtooth border is similar in appearance to a Sawtooth border. The REEL SAMPLER has an appliquéd Dogtooth border. Compare it with the pieced Sawtooth border on the WHIG ROSE quilt. The Dogtooth bor-

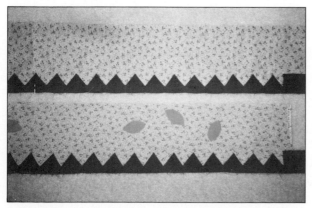

Plate 66. *Machine stitch appliqué pieces to borders before sewing border to quilt top. Photo: Letty Martin.*

der is made of more upright, sharp triangles than the Sawtooth border. The Dogtooth border is frequently seen appliquéd on old nineteeth-century album quilts. It may be seen on both sides of the border, only the inside, or only the outside of the border. It is easy to appliqué. See Figure 44.

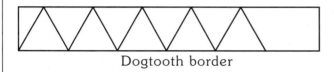

Dogtooth border

Sawtooth border

Figure 44.

Cut a strip of fabric 2¼" wide and about four to six inches longer than the border length. This strip can be pieced and therefore can be cut on the crosswise fabric grain. Press under ¼" on the one lengthwise edge of the fabric strip. See Figure 45.

2¼"   ¼"

Figure 45.

Make a template of the Dogtooth border pattern from template plastic. Place the Dogtooth border template on the right side of the strip with the point on the fold line and mark the Dogtooth design. If the strip was pieced, position the template so this seam will be in a valley of the design. Do not mark the design right to the end of the border strip. Leave the last three to four teeth at each end unmarked. These last few teeth can be marked after the borders are sewn to the quilt, giving you room to stretch them out or squeeze in so they will

fit the space and the corners can all be resolved the same.

Slash the fabric strip down to the V. See Figure 46.

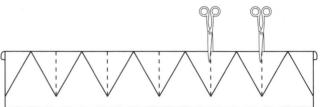

Figure 46.

Press under the edges along the marked Dogtooth lines forming triangles. See Figure 47.

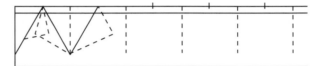

Figure 47.

Fold the border and fabric strip in half to find the center. A tooth or valley should be centered on the border. Pin in place on the border and straight stitch machine appliqué those Dogteeth you have prepared. Sew borders to the quilt top. Mark and appliqué remaining Dogteeth to complete the border. See Plates 69, 70, 71, and 72 for how to resolve corners.

ASSEMBLING YOUR QUILT

Now that your quilt top is completed, it is ready to be assembled. Basting is the process of assembling the three layers in a quilt: the backing, batting, and quilt top. Some tension is needed as you stack these layers and baste them together to keep each smooth and wrinkle free. This tension lets you smoothly assemble the three layers leaving no wrinkles or excess fabric which might interfere with quilting.

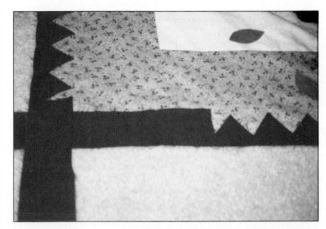

Plate 69. *Photo: Letty Martin.*

Plate 70. *Photo: Letty Martin.*

Plate 71. *Fitting the Dogteeth at the corners. Photo: Letty Martin.*

Plate 72. *Photo: Letty Martin.*

THE QUILT BACKING

Material used for backing the quilt can be a muslin or printed calico. To determine how much backing material you need for your quilt follow these guidelines. The backing should be slightly larger than the quilt top, about two to four inches on each side. Measure the length of your quilt top and add eight inches. A small quilt of 40" wide or less may only require a length of fabric. Quilts wider than 40" will generally need two to three lengths of material sewn together. The length of each backing piece will be the length of the quilt plus the extra eight inches. For example a quilt top measuring 57" x 64" would need four yards of backing material. To the 64" length add 8" which equals 72" or 2 yards. Double this yardage to four yards of material for backing this quilt.

The four yard piece of material will be folded in half lengthwise and cut. Use a pin to mark the upper edge of each length of material. See Figure 48, on page 146.

Remove the selvages and sew the two-yard edges together using a ¼" seam allowance, with the top (the edge with the pins) at the same end. This will ensure that any shading in the fabric or printed design running in a specific direction will be uniform over both halves of the backing fabric.

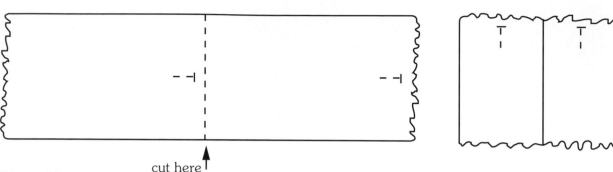

cut here

Figure 48.

Press seam allowances to one side.

The backing fabric is now approximately 84" wide. This will be wide enough for many quilts. In our example, we will need 65" of backing fabric (57" width plus 8" extra). Our fabric is now wider than needed. We will need to cut 9½" from each side to make our backing fabric 65" wide (84" - 65" = 19" divided by 2 = 9½").

Fold the backing fabric into quarters and with a safety pin mark the side centers and end centers of the backing. This will help center the quilt top when layering.

If your quilt top is wider than 90", you will need three lengths of fabric. Divide the fabric in thirds and cut apart. Once again, mark the upper edges with pins, remove selvages, and sew the three pieces of fabric together. The quilt top would be centered on the piece of fabric and any excess width removed equally from each side.

Muslin, both bleached and unbleached, is available in 90" and 108" width. Also 90" wide pastel printed fabrics are available. Using the wider fabrics would eliminate your having to sew together lengths of fabric and quilt through seam allowances.

As mentioned earlier, the backing should be slightly larger than the quilt top, about two to four inches on each side. This extra fabric is used to hold the backing in place while you are basting the quilt. After the basting process is completed this extra backing fabric can be folded over the quilt's edges and pinned in place to protect the edges while the quilt is being quilted. This will prevent the batting from getting thin around the quilt's edges as well as give a neat look to your quilt while being quilted. Unpin the backing and it will give the hoop some extra fabric to grip as you quilt the borders.

LAYERING A QUILT
There are several ways a quilt can be layered. One way is to pull taut and pin the backing to carpeting; another is to tape it to a vinyl floor or a table top (if the quilt top is small). You can also drape the backing over a table top or use wooden stretcher bars. All these methods offer some means of stretching the backing and providing a wrinkle free surface upon which to spread the batting and stretch the quilt top. Choose the method which best suits the space and materials available in your home.

Wooden stretcher bars are easy to prepare and use at home. Stretcher bars let you baste the quilt while working at a comfortable height. To make your own set of stretcher bars, you will need four clear pine 1" x 2" boards in lengths slightly longer than the top you are basting. You will need two pair of boards – two boards of each length. These clear pine 1 x 2's can be purchased at your local lumber yard. Clear pine means the wood is free from knot holes and is therefore stronger than wood with knot holes. Stretcher bar lengths that are most useful are 4, 6, 8, and 10 feet long. Buy two boards of each length you wish to use. This assortment of stretcher bars will let you stretch most of the quilts you might make. The bars are used in pairs, and you can use the pairs closest in size to your quilt top, yet larger than it.

Prepare the bars to use as follows. Prepare a sleeve of fabric which will be stapled to the full length of the stretcher bar. The fabric should be about five inches wide. Sew fabrics lengths together until they equal that of the stretcher bar. Fold the strip of fabric in half lengthwise, with wrong sides together. Press to the wrong side ½" on the raw edges. Sew together on the sewing machine. Match the centers of the board and fabric, lapping the sewn edges of the fabric over the board ⅝", so that the folded edge extends away from the board. See Figure 49.

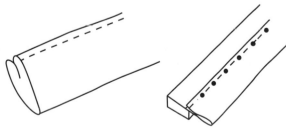

Figure 49.

Working from the center out toward the ends, use an electric staple gun or hammer and tacks to attach the fabric to the stretcher bar, about ½" to ⅝" in from the

edge of the wood the length of the board. Mark the centers of each board with a permanent marker. Every four inches make a long mark and at two inches a short mark. These marks will help to evenly get the quilt in the frame. Prepare all four boards this way. See Figure 50.

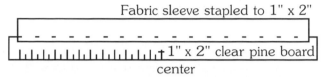

Fabric sleeve stapled to 1" x 2"

1" x 2" clear pine board
center

Figure 50.

Four C-clamps will be used to hold the boards together when stretching the quilt. A 3" C-clamp is a good size if you will be purchasing them. You will need four wood kitchen chairs for the stretcher bar frame to rest upon as it is assembled. To use the stretcher bars, lay the longest boards parallel, with the fabric edge facing the center of the frame and about as far apart as the width of your quilt backing. Rest the bars on the chair backs. Have the chair seats facing each other. Now put the second set of bars across the top and at the ends of the long bars, fabric sleeve facing inward. They should be about as far apart as the quilt backing is long. Secure the boards where they meet at each corner with a C-clamp. See Plate 73.

Plate 73. *Photo: Letty Martin.*

To use the stretcher bars, start by pinning the center edges of the length and width of the quilt backing to the center of the fabric sleeve on each stretcher bar. Working from the centers out toward the corners, pin every three to four inches, placing pins parallel with the stretcher bar. Use the long straight pins. Overlap the quilt backing and fabric sleeve about ½". The wrong side of the backing will be facing up. When all four sides are pinned you can add tension if needed and square the frame. See Plate 74.

Plate 75. *Check to make sure corners are square. Photo: Letty Martin.*

Plate 74. *Photo: Letty Martin.*

Adjust the stretcher bars as necessary at this time to place tension on the backing fabric. Loosen the C-clamps and move the bars closer together or farther apart as needed. Be sure the corners of the stretcher bars are square. Use a quilter's square ruler to see if the corners of the frame are square. See Plate 75.

Once the backing is stretched and square go back and add more straight pins filling in between the pins already in place. Pull the backing to stretch it as you are pinning.

Unwrap the batting and place it over the backing. If it is larger than the backing have one end and side even with the backing and the excess extending over the other two edges. If the batting is close in size to the quilt backing, you can center the batting on the backing. Carefully smooth out the wrinkles and fold lines. Work the excess fullness out toward each edge or toward the edges extending over the backing edges if the batting is larger than the backing. Trim off the excess batting even with the backing.

Check your quilt top before placing over the batting. Make sure all loose threads are trimmed. Make sure dark seam allowances are narrower than the light seam allowances so they will not show through light fabrics. Trim off the dark seams a little if they show. And finally carefully press your quilt top before stretching.

Place the quilt top, right side up, over the batting. The top should be centered on the backing with the center of the ends and sides matching those of the backing. This will let any seams in the backing be centered in relation to the quilt top and parallel with its edges. Begin to pin the quilt top through the other two layers, first at the top and bottom centers, then the side edges. Pull to put some tension on the quilt top. Pin through all three layers. Use the long quilter's straight pins, pinning parallel with the quilt edges. Once again pin from the center toward the corners. Put a few pins on one side of the quilt, then go to the other side and pin opposite the first pins. See Plate 76.

Plate 76. *Pinning the quilt top to batting and backing. Photo: Letty Martin.*

Put pins about 3" to 4" apart. Once the quilt is square and stretched, add brass safety pins in between the straight pins along the quilt edges.

You are now ready to begin basting the quilt top. Basting with small brass safety pins goes fast and they hold the layers secure. Using size 0 brass safety pins, pin every 3" to 4". Try to place pins in areas you will not be quilting. Pin as far in as you can reach on all four sides. You will use 12 to 16 pins for every square foot of surface. A small quilt of 3' x 4' would need 144

brass safety pins. There are 12 square feet in the quilt multiplied by 12 pins per square foot equaling 144. This gives you a guide as to the approximate number of pins needed to pin baste a small quilt. Large quilts can use 500 to 700 brass safety pins!

When you cannot reach any more unpinned areas, you are ready to roll the end stretcher bars. Unpin the backing along the side stretcher bars about 18" on opposite sides but the same end of the quilt. See Plate 77. With a helper, release the C-clamps and roll the end stretcher bar under. Roll the quilt smoothly under to the area where the top is unpinned. Replace and tighten the C-clamps making sure the corners are once again square. See Plate 78.

Plate 77. *Photo: Letty Martin.*

Plate 78. *Rolling the bars in opposite directions. Photo: Letty Martin.*

Repeat at the other end. However, this time roll the end stretcher bar over the top. See Plate 79.

Plate 79. *Continuing the basting. Photo: Letty Martin.*

Rolling one bar under and the other over helps keep an even tension on the quilt top. Pin baste as far as you can reach and repeat rolling the end stretcher bars as often as necessary until the quilt top is all pin basted. Usually rolling each end twice is about all that is needed.

Unpin the backing from the stretcher bars. The extra margin of backing can be folded over the quilt's edges and pinned in place with the brass safety pins. Now the quilting begins. Quilting brings life to your quilt!

MARKING QUILTING DESIGNS

The quilting design is marked on the top after the quilt has been stretched if it is to be quilted in a hoop. Mark as the area is to be quilted because the marked designs tend to rub off when handling the quilt. Also how a quilt is to be quilted may be decided as the quilting progresses by marking as you are ready to quilt an area. The Berol® Verithin silver pencil is a good marking device for curved or straight lines. Mark the lines lightly. Straight lines, such as crosshatching or quilting a quarter of an

inch from the seam lines could be indicated with masking tape. Put on the tape and remove it when you finish quilting for the day. Chalk wheels can also be used for marking straight lines.

There are many other marking devices available, but do follow the manufacturer's instructions and test on some scrap fabric before using on your quilt top. Launder the test sample to make sure the marks will come out of your fabric before using on your quilt.

QUILTING

The quilting stitch is a simple running stitch. It holds the three layers of the quilt together. However, quilting is beautiful on its own and adds beauty to the quilt top, giving depth, dimension, and design.

Most people quilt in a hoop or quilt frame. This helps to hold the three layers securely together and will free your hands for quilting. Hoops come in many different shapes and sizes: round, oval, rectangular, or square and half a circle for quilting edges of the quilt. A 16" round hoop is a good size as it will hold a 12" block.

Quilting needles are called betweens. They are a short needle which helps to give small quilting stitches. A number 10 is a good size to begin with. The larger the needle size, the smaller the needle. Some needles of the same size have smaller eyes, so experiment to find a needle size and eye combination you can easily quilt with and thread. A needle threader helps when it is hard to get the needle threaded, especially a needle with a small eye.

Quilting thread is heavier than sewing thread and comes in a variety of colors. Off-white is the most often used color of quilting thread. Use a thread length of about 18" to 20". Cut the thread off the spool on an angle for ease in threading the needle. Thread the needle with the cut end and then make a single knot in that same end. This helps prevent the thread tangling. Always knot the end cut from the spool.

A thimble is needed to protect the middle finger of the right hand from being punctured by the needle. Thimbles come in many sizes, shapes, and are made from many different material. There are plastic, leather, and metal thimbles. Finding a thimble that fits your finger and does not fall off is one of the most important points to consider. If a metal or plastic thimble is used the dimples in the top and sides need to be deep enough to hold the needle and not let it slip.

Begin quilting by inserting the needle, on the front of the quilt, about a half inch away from where the first stitch is to be. The needle will only be between the layers of the quilt, in the batting, coming up where the first stitch begins. Pull gently to pop the knot so it is sandwiched between the fabrics. Gather two or three stitches on the needle and pull it through the layers of the quilt. The left hand is held under the hoop. Use the middle or index finger of the left hand to help feel when the needle has just cleared the bottom layer, then push the needle up and pull it through the fabric with the right hand. Strive to have small even stitches, about 8 to 10 per inch. If you are a new quilter, concentrate on having even stitches, rather than very small stitches since they tend to get smaller the more you quilt. See Figure 51.

When ending a thread, make an over-

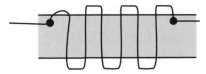

Figure 51. *Strive for even stitches and spacing.*

hand knot in the quilting thread about one half inch from the last stitch. Take a stitch through the quilt top only, as when you began, and pop the knot. Bring the needle up about three quarters of an inch away from where it entered the quilt top. See Figure 52.

Figure 52. *Making an overhand knot.*

BINDING THE QUILT'S EDGES

There are several ways to finish the edges of your quilt now that it is quilted. One finish that is used a lot is to cut a separate binding, sew it on and fold it over the raw edges. The binding also becomes a decorative part of the total quilt. It can be a design element, offering a contrasting color or blending in with the border. A French binding or one that is cut to allow for a double thickness of fabric offers extra protection to the quilt's edges. Since the edges of the quilt are subject to a lot of wear, the double thickness is a practical consideration. Bias binding has the added advantage that the wear along the edge is spread over many different threads, not just one or two as is the case with straight grain binding.

Cutting the binding 2" wide will give a finished edge of ¼" to ⅜" depending on the thickness of the batting. The binding can be cut on the bias or straight grain. Binding cut on the straight grain is suitable for quilts which have straight edges. Slightly less fabric may be needed to bind a quilt using the straight grain. Striped fabrics can be effectively used cut on the crosswise or lengthwise grain line depending on the design you want to create.

To figure how much binding is needed to go around your quilt, measure the length and width. Add those figures together and multiply by two, adding an extra 8" to 10" to cover the corner pleats. Cut enough binding to equal this measurement. Whichever binding you use, bias or straight grain, the 2" wide strips will need to be sewn together to give the total length you need to go around the quilt. Cut the ends of the strips so they are on a 45° angle and parallel with each other. Place right sides together with ends offset ¼" and sew a ¼" seam. Press the seam open. The angle and open seam help to distribute the bulk of the seam, giving a smooth look to your binding. See Figure 53.

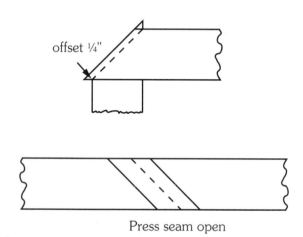

Figure 53. *Joining binding strips.*

Now that the binding is one length, press it lengthwise with wrong sides together. Place the raw edges of the binding next to the raw edges on the front of the quilt. The folded edge of the binding will be facing the center of the quilt. Begin sewing along one side of the top. Leave a 6" tail of the binding free as you begin to sew. Sew toward a corner, stopping exactly ¼" from the edge. Back stitch and cut the threads. Fold the binding up on a 45° angle so that its edge is now parallel with the next edge

of the quilt to be bound. Fold the binding down leaving a pleat the width of the seam allowance, ¼". Begin sewing ¼" from the edge. Back stitch. Continue toward the next corner and repeat the above steps. See Figure 54.

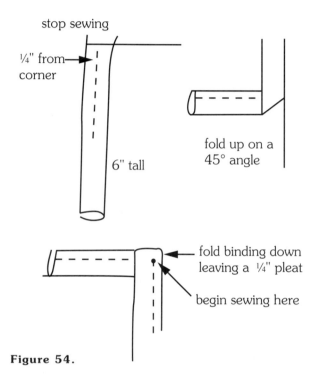

Figure 54.

Stop sewing about 6" from where the ends of the binding will meet. Cut your thread. Overlap the binding ends with the beginning end on the bottom. Pin. Follow the diagram to make a 45° angle that will let the ends meet exactly filling the remaining space. To transfer, the angle of the beginning strip to the end of the binding strip, mark the angle's corners with a pencil dot on the edges of the end binding strip. Open the end strip and connect the dots. Measure and mark a line ½" away toward the extra binding, for seam allowance. Cut off the excess binding. Sew the two binding edges together. Press seam open. Fold in half and finish sewing binding to the quilt.

You will not be able to tell where the binding begins or ends. See Figure 55.

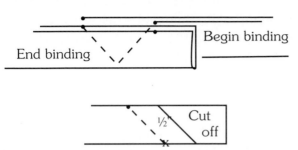

Figure 55. *Joining the beginning and ending of binding.*

Now fold the binding to the back of the quilt and catch in place with a small tack or blind hem stitch. Thread color should match the binding. You will be able to miter the corners by just folding. As you sew the binding on, sew the miters in place with a couple of invisible stitches.

Border edges that have scallops, curved corners, or other curved areas need a bias binding. A bias binding has the flexibility to bend around these curves. The quilt FLORAL MEDALLION has scalloped edges. Cutting a bias binding takes more fabric than cutting a binding on the straight grain of the fabric. Cut a bias binding that is 2" wide. About ¾ to 1¼ yard of fabric will be needed to cut binding for a twin to king size quilt. A large piece of fabric means fewer seams joining the strips of fabric. Cut strips 2" wide, joining the ends on a 45° angle into one long strip, long enough to go around your quilt. Slightly more yardage will be needed to go around the scalloped edges. Refer to the above directions for figuring how much binding to go around a quilt and add an extra three feet to those figures. If a quilt with straight edges needed 9 yards of binding one of the same size with scalloped edges would need an additional 3 feet or a total of 12 yards of binding.

Place the right side of the bias to the right side of the quilt top, raw edges even. Start sewing on one side of a curve, not in a corner. Begin sewing about four inches from the beginning of the bias. See Figure 56.

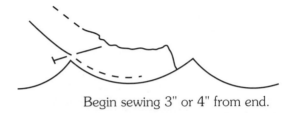

Begin sewing 3" or 4" from end.

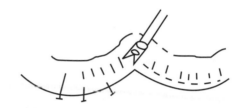

Figure 56.

As you are sewing around the curves, do not stretch the binding. Inner corners will need to be clipped ³⁄₁₆" so the binding will go on smoothly.

With a straight pin mark the top of the inside corner, just beyond the clip in the seam allowance. Sew up to the pin stopping with the sewing machine needle down, straighten the fabric edge by rearranging the quilt and continue sewing. Stop sewing three or four inches before reaching where you began sewing. Overlap the ends of the bias strips. Mark the beginning position on the end tail as described above. As you hand sew the binding to the back of the quilt, a small tuck needs to be sewn in the binding so it will lie flat on the inside corners of the scallops. To miter the inside corners of the scallops and remove excess fabric follow these steps.
1. Fold binding in half exactly opposite the inside corner.

2. Using a second needle, sew a small right angle triangle in the binding. See Figure 57.

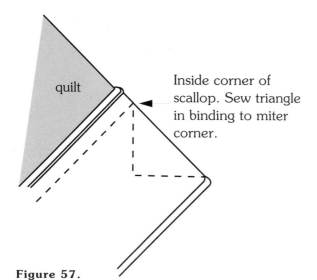

quilt

Inside corner of scallop. Sew triangle in binding to miter corner.

Figure 57.

3. Turn the binding to the back of the quilt and continue sewing binding on. As you come to another inside corner of the scallop, repeat the above process.

4. The binding will lie flat where the tuck is formed.

MAKE AN EASY PILLOW

Any quilt block can be made into a pillow. Pillows make nice gifts or decorator items for your home. After a quilt block is quilted this is a simple way to make it into an envelope-style pillow. An envelope pillow has a back that is made in two sections which overlap in the middle. The pillow form is slipped in place through the overlap. Use a pillow form one size larger than your pillow size. If your pillow measures 15" square, then use a 16" square pillow form. Using a slightly larger size pillow form gives a nice full pillow with firm corners.

Follow these instructions to make your pillow. Measure the quilt block. Our exam- ple measures 15½" square. The backing pieces will be cut the width of the pillow, 15½" by half the length, plus an overlap allowance. To figure out this measurement, divide the length of one side in half, 15½" divided by 2 = 7¾". To this number add 3½" for the overlap and hem. 7¾" plus 3½" = 11¼". You will cut two pillow backing pieces 15½" x 11¼".

Hem one 15½" long edge of each pillow back piece. There is a 1½" hem allowance. First fold under ½" to the wrong side and press. Then fold 1" under, press and sew. See Figure 58.

Figure 58.

With right sides together, pin a pillow back piece to the quilt block, hemmed edge toward the pillow's center. Next pin the other pillow back piece in place with the hemmed edge toward the center of the pillow and parallel with the first hemmed edge. Use a quarter to round the corners of the pillow before sewing. The corners of the pillow will appear square. Sew all around the pillow square using a ¼" seam allowance. See Figure 59.

Clip excess fabric off seam allowance at

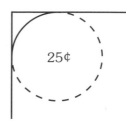

25¢

Figure 59.

corners and turn right side out. Slip pillow form in place.

THE FINISHING TOUCHES

Remember to sign and date your quilt, including any other information you would like to be associated with your quilt. This might include the occasion for which it was made, the person for whom it was made, or your relationship to the recipient. Congratulations on a job well done!

MAIL ORDER SUPPLY SOURCES

Cabin Fever Calicos
P. O. Box 550106
Atlanta, Georgia 30355-2506
1-800-762-2246
Good source of quilting supplies, from fabric to marking devices.

Keepsake Quilting
Route 25 P. O. Box 1618,
Centre Harbor, New Hampshire 03226
1-603-253-8731
Complete source of quilting supplies, including fine nylon thread used for Straight Stitch Machine Applique.

Stearns Technical Textiles Company
100 Williams Street
Cincinnati, Ohio 45215
1-800-345-7150
Order the Mountain Mist Catalog of Classic Quilt Patterns. It contains many patterns, reasonably priced, suitable for Straight Stitch Machine Applique.

BIBLIOGRAPHY

Cunningham, Joe & Gwen Marston. *Creating Feather Designs for the Quilt*. Video, Flint, Michigan: Keva Partnership, 1988.

Dietrich, Mimi. *Happy Endings*. Bothell, Washington: That Patchwork Place, Inc., 1987.

Ferrero, Pat. *Heart and Hands*. San Francisco, California: The Quilt Digest Press, 1987.

Fons, Marianne. *Fine Feathers*. Lafayette, California: C & T Publishing, 1988.

Hall, Carrie A., and Kretsinger, Rose G. *The Romance of the Patchwork Quilt*. New York: Bonanza Books, 1935.

Havig, Bettina. *Missouri Heritage Quilts*. Paducah, Kentucky: American Quilter's Society, 1986.

Holstein, Jonathan. *The Pieced Quilt: An American Design Tradition*. Greenwich, Conn.: New York Graphic Society, LTD., 1973.

Meyer, Suellen. "Early Influences of the Sewing Machine and Visible Machine Stitching on Nineteenth-Century Quilts." *Uncoverings* 1989.

Mountain Mist Catalog of Classic Quilt Patterns. Cincinnati: The Stearns Technical Textiles Co. 1-800-345-7150.

Orlofsy, Patsy and Myron. *Quilts in America*. New York: McGraw Hill Book Co., 1974.

Roberson, Ruth Haislip, ed. *North Carolina Quilts*. Chapel Hill: The University of North Carolina Press, 1988.

Ramsey, Bets, and Waldvogel, MeriKay. *The Quilts of Tennessee. Nashville:* Rutledge Hill Press, 1986.

Simms, Ami. *How to Improve Your Quilting Stitch*. Flint, Michigan: Mallery Press, 1987.

Woodard, Thomas K., and Greenstein, Blanch. *Twentieth Century Quilts*. New York: E. P. Dutton, 1988.

ENDNOTES

1 Pat Ferrero et al., *Heart and Hands* (San Francisco: The Quilt Digest Press, 1987), 38.

2 Ibid., 38.

3 Ibid., 38.

4 Suellen Meyer, "Early Influences of the Sewing Machine and Visible Machine Stitching on Nineteenth-Century Quilts." *Uncoverings 1989* (San Francisco: American Quilt Study Group, 1989), 46.

5 Jonathan Holstein, *The Pieced Quilt: An American Design Tradition* (New York: New York Graphic Society, 1973), 84.

6 Meyer, 46.

7 Meyer, 46.

8 Holstein, 84.

9 Meyer, 48.

10 Bets Ramsey & Merikay Waldvogel, *The Quilts of Tennessee* (Nashville: Rutledge Hill Press, 1986), xvi.

11 Meyer, 45.

12 Ruth Haislip Roberson, ed., *North Carolina Quilts* (Chapel Hill NC: The University of North Carolina Press, 1988), 67.

13 Roberson, 116.

14 Roberson, 116.

15 Patricia Cox Crews & Ronald C. Naugle, *Nebraska Quilts and Quiltmakers* (Lincoln: University of Nebraska Press, 1991), 92, 93.

16 Marshal MacDowell & Ruth D. Fitzgerald, *Michigan Quilts: 150 Years of a Textile Tradition* (East Lansing, MI : Michigan State University, 1987), 83.

17 Roberson, 73.

18 Bettina Havig, *Missouri Heritage Quilts* (Paducah: The American Quilter's Society, 1986), 13.

19 Meyer, 48.

∼ American Quilter's Society ∼
dedicated to publishing books for today's quilters

These books can be found in local bookstores and quilt shops. If you are unable to locate a title in your area, you can order by mail from AQS, P.O. Box 3290, Paducah, KY 42002-3290.
Please add $1 for the first book and 40¢ for each additional one to cover postage and handling.
(International orders please add $1.50 for the first book and $1 for each additional one.)